BRITAIN IN OLD PHOTOGRAPHS

GLOUCESTERSHIRE AT WORK

STEPHEN MILLS

SUTTON PUBLISHING LIMITED

Sutton Publishing Limited
Phoenix Mill · Thrupp · Stroud
Gloucestershire · GL5 2BU

First published 1997

Copyright © Stephen Mills, 1997

Title page: Remedial work on the Stroudwater
Canal, near Stonehouse, *c.* 1910.

British Library Cataloguing in Publication Data
A catalogue record for this book is available from the
British Library.

ISBN 0-7509-1552-8

Typeset in 10/12 Perpetua.
Typesetting and origination by
Sutton Publishing Limited.
Printed in Great Britain by
Ebenezer Baylis, Worcester.

Dedicated to my wife, Liz. For her patience, constant help and attention to
detail throughout the preparation of this book.

CONTENTS

Loaded lorries at William Gardner's milling engineering company, Gloucester, *c.* 1930.

INTRODUCTION

Every region has its own range of trades and industries. However, in the case of Gloucestershire, this range remained remarkably wide for centuries. Alongside the more usual activities that were essentially universal, such as farming and corn milling, a great diversity of trades and industries developed within the county at different times. Often, localized conditions were instrumental in the development of a new trade.

Gloucestershire comprises three distinctly different regions, namely the Forest of Dean, the Severn Vale and the Cotswolds. The differing characteristics of each led inevitably to specialization, each region developing its own particular crafts, trades and manufacturers. Alongside such specialities were many occupations, especially those related to agriculture and the rural crafts, that were encountered everywhere. There were also the blacksmith, cobbler, village builder and grocer, to name but a few, trades encountered anywhere that people lived together in any significant number.

In terms of the county's industrial and manufacturing past, three areas predominated, namely the Forest of Dean, the Stroud valleys and the City of Gloucester itself. The presence of iron and coal deposits in the once-isolated Forest ensured that thriving mining and industrial communities developed in the region. Alongside these, many occupations were based on the use of the Forest's other main resources of timber and stone. Both were exploited over many centuries, providing a stable way of life for local inhabitants.

In contrast, the Cotswolds remained largely agricultural in nature, untouched by industrial development. However, where suitable, the characteristic limestone was quarried and streams harnessed to power small corn mills. As elsewhere in the small Cotswold towns and villages, traditional occupations and crafts provided work for the inhabitants.

In Stroud and the five valleys radiating out from it were, from the Middle Ages onward, innumerable water-powered mills that formed the heart of the county's woollen cloth manufacturing industry. Here, the making of cloth touched virtually the entire population and formed the mainstay of the local economy over several centuries. Ultimately, its presence shaped much of the social, economic and physical configuration of the region. Further south, other cloth mills provided employment in and around the towns of Wotton-under-Edge, Kingswood and Charfield. Many major engineering companies in the region developed to meet the needs of the local cloth trade.

The City of Gloucester was the other main industrial centre, situated at what became the hub of a network of crucially important transport links. The city stood at a major crossing point over the Severn and at the intersections of important roads, canals and railway lines. These enabled raw materials to be imported easily into the heart of the city and for finished goods to be moved rapidly to their destinations. In and around Gloucester, manufacturers produced a bewildering assortment of products ranging from pins and matches to railway waggons, steam engines and aircraft. Near the centre stood the city's docks, linked by the Gloucester–Sharpness Canal and the River Severn to markets, both national and international.

Society's requirements constantly change with time and this is inevitably reflected in its manufacturing base. As a consequence, there has always been a tendency for one industry to fade and be replaced by another one. Thus, in Stroud, the cloth trade dwindled and many of the redundant mills were taken over by newer industries, happy to capitalize on the cheap factory space and available workforce. In Gloucester, the manufacture of railway rolling stock, aircraft and much of the heavy engineering that had made the city famous gradually disappeared. Once again, new industries moved into the area. For instance, in the late 1950s British Nylon Spinners took over part of the redundant Gloucester Aircraft site at Brockworth, providing employment for thousands. At about the same time, Permali were opening their huge new works along the Bristol Road, an area already packed with manufacturing sites, timber yards, Morelands match factory, Simon-Barrons mill engineering works, Gloucester Carriage & Wagon Works, and Fielding & Platt's Atlas engineering works, to name but a few. In among these ran a web of railway branch lines along which small locomotives shuttled materials back and forth around the clock.

Much like the surrounding smaller towns and villages, in former days the city was self-sufficient in many ways. There was little that could not be made within or close to the city boundaries. In addition, for many years it also had its own power station, first in Blackfriars and latterly at Castle Mead, and its own flour mills dotted around the docks. What could not be manufactured in the vicinity could be brought in via one of the many transport systems that met in the city.

Such has been the range in both type and scale of the county's trades and industries that no single volume could hope to encompass all of them. What this book attempts to do is to give a flavour of this diversity, where many specialized crafts and professions were carried on alongside those that were to be encountered throughout the land. In some instances, trades still continue, albeit in much changed and modernized forms, whereas in others they have faded away and are no more than distant memories. Change has been a constant theme throughout Gloucestershire's working past. Long periods of stability have been followed by either gradual evolution or sudden alterations in working patterns. This was perfectly summarized in a trade publication of 1904 which noted the effects of newer sources of power on manufacturing:

The changes and changing methods brought by steam and electricity have revolutionised industrial conditions here, as elsewhere. In this change, Gloucestershire in some industries has yielded the palm to more fortunate competitors, in some she has gained the supremacy formerly claimed by other localities. But fortunately, with the change in form of industry has come an equally marked improvement in character and quantity. To-day, not only a large number, but a larger proportion, of Gloucestershire's population are engaged in some form of manufacturing than ever before, while the product of their brains and hands was never in higher repute.

It is hoped that in its way, this modest book will help to illustrate the roots of some of Gloucestershire's most important occupations, trades and industries, and act as a visual reminder of some of the activities that provided employment for many of the present generation's parents and grandparents.

TIMBER & TIMBER PRODUCTS

Throughout the county's history, timber has been an important commodity, one that was used in the construction of every cottage, mill and factory. In earlier centuries, timber was often used close to where it had been grown, with the village carpenter sourcing his timber from local woods and sawing it by hand in his own saw-pit. However, from the eighteenth century, Gloucester began to assume an increasingly important role in the timber trade, with supplies being brought into the city by water. Particularly after the Gloucester–Sharpness Canal was opened, linking the city's docks with those at Sharpness, increasing tonnages of timber began to pour into yards set up adjacent to the docks and, in the 1850s, new yards created next to the canal, along the Bristol Road leading out of the city. Some timber boats came directly to Gloucester via the canal, while larger vessels transferred all or part of their load to lighters in the docks at Sharpness.

The country needed increasing amounts of timber for both building and industrial purposes and Gloucester became an important centre for the trade, with supplies coming in from Europe, Scandinavia, the Baltic region, and North and South America. By the middle of the nineteenth century, the timber trade was one of the most important of Gloucester's industries. By the end of the century, the city was the country's ninth largest timber importing centre, no mean feat considering Gloucester's inland location. It was estimated that, including workers engaged in transportation, around 7,000 local workers made their livings from the trade.

Despite the inevitable ups and downs, the trade thrived and, as part of an expansion programme in the 1890s, a timber pond was built in Monk Meadow. There were a number of timber yards spread out along the bank of the canal running parallel with the Bristol Road, a handful of which were to be very long-lived. Of these, three companies stood out: Price, Walker & Co., Nicks & Co., and Joseph Griggs.

Price, Walker's roots lay in the eighteenth century, the trade being established by Morgan Price in the 1730s. The company was reconfigured on a number of occasions and was run by a succession of Price family members, becoming a limited company in 1889. By the dawn of the present century, the company was operating from a 20-acre site littered with stockpiles, sawmills and drying mills. Each year 100,000 tons of timber came in from Russia, Sweden, Canada, Prussia, Austria, and the Gulf of Mexico to be sawn and prepared in the company's mills; the main sawmill had been built in 1894. Much was shipped from Sharpness in the company's own lighters. Completed timber products were sent on to customers, primarily by rail or water, the site being connected to both the LMS and GWR railways. At one time, over 700 hands were employed by the company.

Nicks & Co. grew out of a small company set up by William Nicks in 1840, the original base of operations being in High Orchard, near the docks. 1870 saw expansion and relocation to a 7-acre site along the Bristol Road. Company specialities included vacuum impregnation of timber with creosote. As with some of the other importers, a considerable volume of its business was conducted with the railway companies, with huge numbers of sleepers being supplied. Apart from this, the company used its steam sawmills to turn out large quantities of finished timber that was exported throughout the country. Timber had formerly come by canal, imported from a multitude of overseas suppliers.

The company set up by Joseph Griggs originated in Loughborough in the 1890s and was joined subsequently by an offshoot in West Hartlepool. Within a few years, the company had relocated to Gloucester, primarily as the city formed the nearest inland port to major markets in Birmingham and other parts of the industrial Midlands. Timber arrived mainly by lighter from Sharpness, supplies coming in from around the world. As well as timber, the company also specialized in supplying slate from a number of sources. Latterly, some timber also came via a dedicated rail spur which ran directly from the local industrial rail network into the yard. Thus, in terms of transport, like the other local timber firms, Griggs' yard was well supplied with water, road and rail links.

Not all the timber trade relied on imported woods and all areas of the county had their own timber fellers and preparers. Some were larger than others and a number comprised family enterprises of remarkable longevity. For instance, in the Stroud region and the Cotswolds, the timber company of Denis Brown continues to operate, having been originally founded by a notable Yorkshire farming family. The associated timber business was set up in the 1890s and continues in Woodchester to this day.

Close to Brown's timber yard at Woodchester is the site, now occupied by a chemical company, of one of the largest timber mills in the Stroud district, the sawmills of Henry Workman. Originally set up in 1870, the company survived up to 1957. The bustling business operated its own steam cranes that ran on the company's own tracks and that of the Midland Railway. For decades, Workman's remained the largest timber business in the region, much of the timber coming from relatively local sources. Later, the company was responsible for hauling much timber with its own transport, although some was contracted out to Brunsdons. Over the years, they used horses, followed by steam traction, and finally Foden diesel trucks for much of this work. For a time in the 1890s, part of the works also made walking sticks, one of the peculiarities of the Stroud valleys. Although Workman was not alone in the business, the company outlived many of its competitors.

For a long time, horses operated alongside steam power, with teams often being used to move enormous loads. This six-horse team of the Brown family is in the process of moving a large trunk from local woods.

A team pauses outside the gates to Woodchester Park, near Nympsfield, with a relatively light load, early 1920s. The timber probably came from Selsley Woods.

A six-horse team of the Brown family at work, timber-hauling in Sherborne Park, near Northleach, probably in the 1920s.

The long-established Woodchester timber business of Denis Brown Ltd had its roots in Leyburn, North Yorkshire, where the family formerly ran three large farms. The timber business was originally set up in the 1890s. Here, one of the company's traction engines pauses with a load of tree trunks, 1920s. Denis Brown is on the left.

Things in the timber trade did not always go smoothly! In the late 1950s, this Perkins-powered Dodge lorry took a wrong turn in Stroud and became stuck in the narrow Church Street. In order to extricate the load, it proved easier to back up a second lorry and saw off the ends of the trunks.

By the 1960s, steam and horse power had long been abandoned. These three Unipower trucks, parked in Cossack Square, Nailsworth, formed part of Brown's timber-hauling fleet. These rugged trucks could traverse almost any terrain and were capable of hauling huge loads.

An exceptionally early picture showing Mr William Nicks, founder of the timber business of Nicks & Co., standing in the doorway of the company's first premises in Merchants Road, Gloucester, 1863.

The bustling canal-side timber yard of Nicks & Co., 1890. At this time, most timber arrived by water and the huge stocks of timber were moved almost entirely by hand.

Fire was a constant threat in the timber trade and few businesses escaped unscathed. Nicks' yard was devastated by fire in March 1907. This photograph shows the still-smouldering scene the morning after.

Workers glumly survey the scorched remains of the site's boiler house.

The charred remains of the sawmill's steam engine. Rope drives to power saws etc. were taken off the large flywheel.

Nicks' timber yard, looking across the Bristol Road, 1916. At this time, the site was still in a relatively rural location. All of the surrounding land has since been swallowed up by the expanding city. The Avenue Hotel is now to the right, on the corner of Tuffley Avenue.

Some of the workers employed by Nicks & Co., 1890s. It was not unusual for several generations of the same family to be employed simultaneously.

Unloading timber from the *Ncatira* of Southampton, November 1940. The lighter *Uley* is moored alongside. Huge tonnages were unloaded and transported using a combination of simple cranes and manpower until the 1950s or later.

A busy scene along the banks of the Gloucester–Sharpness Canal in the early 1960s, with timber destined for the Joseph Griggs' yard being unloaded from the *Alexander*. In earlier days, unloading timber was carried out by subcontracting to a foreman who would choose a suitable gang of labourers to unload the boat. Timber was regularly carried at a running pace!

The lower Bristol Road area of Gloucester. Note the various railway lines that linked the Griggs and Nicks timber yards. Another branch veered off to the right, allowing regular weekday coal shipments to reach the Bristol Road gasworks. Usually, LMS Class 4F 0–6–0 engines worked this route, continuing up to the late 1960s. The line running into Griggs' yard originally crossed the canal via a swingbridge. This carried a branch of the Midland Railway into GWR territory. The line operated between 1900 and 1937.

An aerial view, showing the lower Bristol Road area of Gloucester, with Griggs' timber yard in the foreground, adjacent to the canal, November 1961. To its right is the timber business of Nicks & Co.; across the road is the milling engineering works of Simon-Barrons.

Griggs' yard, like most of its peers, was damaged by fire on a number of occasions. One such fire occurred in 1907. Here, the morning after, the *Salamander* fire boat from Gloucester Docks plays water on to the embers. The boat was provided as a joint project between various local timber and corn merchants, the Docks Company and Gloucester Corporation.

In earlier days, timber was moved on from Gloucester's timber yards by combinations of boat, plus horse- and steam-driven road transport. By the 1950s, road transport accounted for most of this work, with merchants using their own lorry fleets to transport timber to various locations. This picture (*c.* 1958) shows one of Joseph Griggs & Co.'s lorries awaiting its next load. Until relatively recently, much timber handling was carried out manually.

The extensive timber yard of Price, Walker & Co., *c.* 1902. This shows the exterior of the main sawmill and the principal timber-cutting bay. Power for the mills came courtesy of a double crank compound condensing steam engine of 450 h.p., built by Woods of Bolton. Summers & Scott of Gloucester also supplied a special engine used to generate electricity for the large site.

The interior of Price, Walker's sawing and planing mill, 1904.

Price, Walker & Co.
LTD.

F. O. CROXFORD, MANAGING DIRECTOR

FOUNDED IN
1736.

INCORPORATED
IN 1889.

TIMBER IMPORTERS, SAWING :: PLANING & MOULDING MILLS TIMBER DRYING PLANT

PORTS :
SHARPNESS DOCKS and GLOUCESTER

HEAD OFFICE :
GLOUCESTER

Telegraphic Address—
PRICE, GLOUCESTER

Telephone—
No. 3013 (3 LINES) GLOUCESTER

This advertisement from the mid-1920s hints at the scale of Price, Walker's timber operations. In 1976, the company celebrated its 240th year and at the time was still importing timber from Canada, Sweden, Finland, Russia, Brazil, West Africa and Malaysia.

Timber retrieved from the forest clearly needs reducing to more manageable sizes. This 1950s picture shows logs being cut and stacked at the Woodgate Sawmill in the Forest of Dean. Variants of the circular saw were the usual method of at least initially reducing wood in size. (From the collection of the Dean Heritage Museum Trust)

Members of the Women's Timber Corps at work at Blaize Bailey, 1942. During the war, many women took over such roles, ones that had formerly been exclusively all-male domains. (From the collection of the Dean Heritage Museum Trust)

In the Stroud region, one of the largest timber firms was that of Henry Workman. The company operated from its sawmill in Woodchester until 1957. This picture from about 1920 illustrates the scale of the business. Large baulks of timber were moved about the site by Workman's own steam cranes.

Inside Workman's mill, tree trunks were reduced to various shapes and sizes. On this line, trunks are being reduced to more manageable profiles by large steam-driven circular saws.

Not surprisingly, the works was damaged by fire on more than one occasion and in April 1911, the main building was gutted. This scene from the morning after shows Stroud fire brigade damping down the remains.

Another scene from the day after, showing how complete was the devastation of the site.

Once a common site in many towns and villages, the wood turner is now largely a thing of the past. Turners made everything from chair legs to ladder rungs to broom and tool handles. They varied enormously in scale, some being sizeable concerns and others one-man affairs. Many of their traditional markets were gradually eroded by the introduction of new materials and manufacturing techniques. This is George Maisey of Ebley, *c.* 1919, in front of his workshop. He had a reputation of being a fine wood turner. Cordwells Garage now occupies the site.

The individual wood turner gradually lost ground to specialist firms such as James Constance & Sons of Longhope. The company was originally founded in 1788 and later advertised under the banner of 'steam turning and joining'. In this early 1960s picture, an operator is turning out countless ladder rungs. The company also made innumerable tool handles. (From the collection of the Dean Heritage Museum Trust)

Here, a worker is engaged in drilling holes in broomheads at Constance's works in Longhope, *c.* 1960. During its working life, Constance's made handles for mops, brooms, brushes, hammers, sledges, spades, shovels, washing dollies, and even cider bungs. Handles were often sent to Sheffield where appropriate blades were fitted. (From the collection of the Dean Heritage Museum Trust)

A general view of organized chaos in J. Constance & Sons' turnery. The works eventually housed a wide range of circular and band saws, drills and many turning machines. The company finally closed its doors in 1983. (From the collection of the Dean Heritage Museum Trust)

The extensive furniture factory of J.A. Matthews & Co., High Orchard, near Gloucester Docks, c. 1920. First established in 1863, the company was built up from a small furniture business originally situated at the corner of Southgate and Parliament Streets. The new factory was built in 1894 on the site of buildings formerly used by the timber firm of Price, Walker & Co.

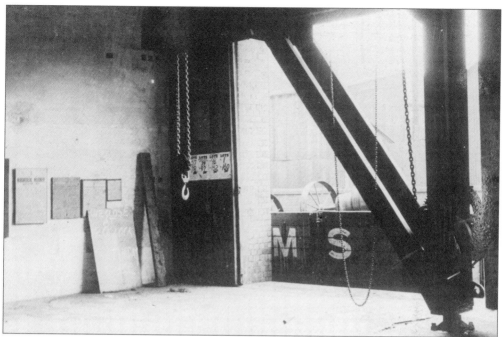

The highly automated factory complex eventually included its own wharf, timber yards, sawmill, warehouses, cabinet-making and upholstery departments, and rail links. Here, an LMS waggon waits for its next load. Small MR Class OF 0–4–0T tank engines operated throughout the docks. Matthews & Co. employed over 200 workers by 1900 and was one of the largest wholesale furniture manufacturers in the country.

Part of the Matthews furniture factory complex. A huge range of products, some patented, were produced and shipped throughout Britain by road and rail. A more traditional form of transport waits patiently outside the offices of J. Romans & Sons, another long-established Gloucester company.

One unusual trade carried on adjacent to Beards Mill in Leonard Stanley was the growing of withies for the manufacture of cricket bats. The business was carried on by Mr Winterbotham of nearby Stonehouse Court. This is believed to be the owner examining part of the crop. The business operated in the 1920s and '30s. The foreman, Edgar Watts, moved to Bungay in Suffolk and carried on in the same line.

A view of Winterbotham's withy beds, taken from the railway viaduct that looms over the site. The beds were watered via a network of small stone-lined channels and sluice gates, fed from the Frome. Many still survive, now buried in deep undergrowth.

One of the largest manufacturers of walking sticks and umbrella handles in the Stroud area was H.S. Hack, whose works were in Bourne Mill, near Stroud. The mill site had been in use from the sixteenth century and had, at times, been a cloth mill, corn mill, shoddy (cheap cloth) manufactory, and cabinet works. Hack's stick business occupied the mill from 1912 up to the 1960s. The company produced a bewildering range of sticks and handles, and made use of a wide range of woods and other materials for their manufacture. Much of its output was exported. This picture shows a consignment of umbrella sticks on its way to overseas markets, *c.* 1935.

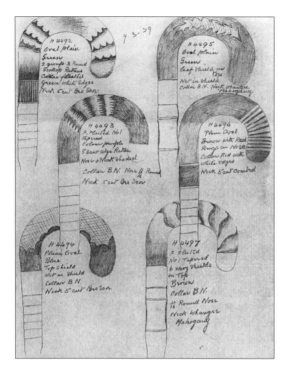

From the start of the business, Hack's kept details of orders in large pattern books. This page from a 1939 entry gives details of various colours and patterns used for a particular range of handles.

Part of the bending and cane shop of the Chalford Stick Company, St Marys Mill, Chalford, 1904. One of the largest stick-making concerns in the district, the company supplied a wide range of products, including umbrella, sunshade and walking sticks, to both British and overseas markets. Branch warehouses or agencies were maintained in London, Manchester, Glasgow, Paris and Berlin.

BREWING & CIDER MAKING

For many years, the small brewery was a common feature in both urban and rural landscapes. It could almost be guaranteed that there was at least one working brewery in virtually all towns and many villages throughout the county. Often, these were very localized affairs, perhaps supplying a handful of pubs in the immediate vicinity. Such was the case with the Royal William at Cranham. This doubled as both pub and brewery and apart from supplying its own needs, distributed beer as far as Brockworth. However, as the nineteenth century progressed, a number of the county's breweries expanded dramatically, primarily through acquisition and mergers with other small brewers. Takeovers and mergers were a constant theme during the first half of the present century. For instance, the modest brewery at the Royal William was acquired by the Stroud-based Godsells Brewery in about 1904.

The two main examples of breweries that expanded through acquisition were what eventually became Whitbreads, in Cheltenham, and the Stroud Brewery, both of which gathered up other brewing concerns both within the county and further afield. Inevitably, such rationalizations within the brewing industry resulted in the demise of many of the smaller, outlying breweries.

Apart from the huge Cheltenham-based Whitbread concern, few of the traditional smaller brewers survive, although in recent years, modest breweries have reopened in villages such as Uley. One family-run brewery that has survived in the county through all these changes has been the Arkell family's Donington Brewery, which still supplies pubs and hotels over a substantial area. All of the others are now no more than memories.

An engraving of the Nailsworth Brewery, *c.* 1890, showing a scene of great activity. The brewery was started in about 1840 by Joseph and Samuel Clissold, later becoming Joseph Clissold & Son. It was eventually taken over by the Cheltenham Original Brewery in 1908 and was closed two years later.

The Brimscombe Brewery was typical of many of the small to medium-sized breweries that once flourished throughout Gloucestershire. It was operated by Smith & Sons at Far Thrupp, near Stroud, from 1856 until about 1918. Sadly, nothing now remains.

An advertisement of about 1900 showing what became one of the largest breweries in the region. The Whitbread Brewery in Cheltenham has one of the longest pedigrees in Gloucestershire. Its origins lie in breweries started in 1760 by Mr Gardner of Cheltenham and Mr Leversage of Middle Lypiatt, although the latter eventually moved his business to Stroud. Gardner's Brewery (later the Original Brewery) gradually grew and, in 1897, took over the Cheltenham Steam Brewery. Its rise continued and over the next thirty years, the company took over rival breweries in Nailsworth, Stow-on-the-Wold, Northleach, Gloucester, Wickwar and Evesham. In 1945, it also acquired the Hereford & Tredegar Brewery, becoming Cheltenham & Hereford Breweries Ltd. In 1959, the company merged with the Stroud Brewery. (The Whitbread Archive)

This picture from before the turn of the century shows the extensive maltings of Gardner's Original Brewery. The various carts and waggons are decked out for an unknown festive occasion, possibly Queen Victoria's Diamond Jubilee in 1897. (The Whitbread Archive)

Workers at Stroud Brewery during the Second World War. Leversage and his two partners moved their business to Stroud and in 1897, took over the Playnes' Minchinhampton Brewery. Under various combinations of owners, the growing business went on to acquire other brewing firms in Marlborough, Malmesbury, Tetbury and eventually, the substantial Godsells' concern in Stroud in 1928. (The Whitbread Archive)

Cask washing, Stroud Brewery, c. 1955, one of the many 'forgotten' but important stages involved in brewing beer. At one time, Stroud Brewery supplied 460 inns, hotels and off licences. (The Whitbread Archive)

A picture of Bown's long-established mineral waterworks in Lansdown, Stroud, *c.* 1900. The works produced a range of mineral and aerated water, very popular at the time.

A regular scene up to the middle of the present century. Here, the Willetts family of the Forest of Dean are making cider, *c.* 1920. The scratter mill comprised a pair of contra-rotating rollers/shredders used to crush apples fed in from the top. They were usually driven off a portable steam or later, diesel or petrol engine. Although many farms produced cider exclusively for their own consumption using their own equipment, there were also itinerant cider makers who travelled from farm to farm, bringing portable equipment with them. Sometimes one particular farmer carried out the work for his neighbours. (From the collection of the Dean Heritage Museum Trust)

The sad remains of an early cider press abandoned to the elements on a farm at Uckington, near Stoke Orchard. Notice the all-wooden screw and massive upper beam.

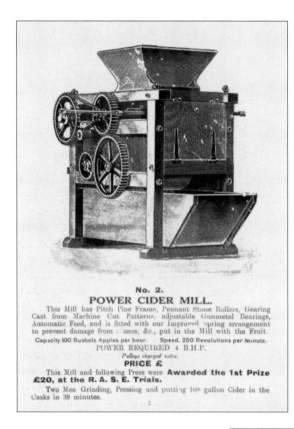

No. 2.
POWER CIDER MILL.

This Mill has Pitch Pine Frame, Pennant Stone Rollers, Gearing Cast from Machine Cut Patterns, adjustable Gunmetal Bearings, Automatic Feed, and is fitted with our Improved spring arrangement to prevent damage from stones, &c., put in the Mill with the Fruit.

Capacity 100 Bushels Apples per hour.　　Speed. 250 Revolutions per Minute.

POWER REQUIRED 4 B.H.P.

Pulleys charged extra.

PRICE £

This Mill and following Press were **Awarded the 1st Prize £20, at the R. A. S. E. Trials.**

Two Men Grinding, Pressing and putting 108 gallon Cider in the Casks in 39 minutes.

One of the most important manufacturers of cider-making equipment in Britain was Workman's of Slimbridge. The company produced a range of presses and mills that were exported throughout the country, often via the railway at Coaley Junction. This advertisement from about 1900 shows a powered 'scratter' mill, used to crush apples.

No. 9.

COMBINED MACHINE.

Power Mill (No. 4) and Quadruple Gear Press (No. 3)

mounted on Wheels and Shafts Complete.

PRICE £

Hand Power Mill No. 4A and No. 3A PRESS

PRICE £

Pulley and Cloths extra.

A Workman's combined scratter mill and press, mounted on a truck. Such units were frequently moved from farm to farm during the season. Power could be provided by any form of steam or internal combustion engine.

TEXTILES

Several textiles were processed within the county at different times in its history, although some were significantly more important than others. Of mainly local importance was flax. Thomas Beale Brown – farmer, sheep rearer, machinery inventor and flax grower – built a flax mill at Hampen on the Cotswolds in 1850. Here, he developed methods for producing materials made from flax and hemp, some of the former being coated with gutta percha (natural rubber secretions). Flax was also grown on clay land around Moreton-in-Marsh where for over a century, linen-weaving formed an important source of employment. First established in 1742, the business of the Busby family carried on up to about 1880, when their weaving factory closed.

Undoubtedly the major player in the field of textiles was the woollen cloth trade. Originally found in cottages in every town, village and hamlet, the trade eventually gravitated to the villages in the valleys radiating out from Stroud. The main reason for the trade's development in this region was the availability of water power. This provided the power for over 200 small fulling and gig mills that ultimately packed the main streams flowing along the valley floors, plus virtually every spring and tributary capable of supplying sufficient water to drive a waterwheel. As the nineteenth century progressed, there was a trend towards fewer but much larger, increasingly mechanized mills. The overall number of mills diminished significantly. This trend continued through the nineteenth century and into the twentieth century. However, as the trade declined and cloth mills were left vacant, numerous other trades and industries moved in to capitalize on the inexpensive accommodation and readily available workforce. One important successor industry was the silk trade, with a number of redundant woollen cloth mills being turned over to silk throwing. For a time, some silk weaving was carried on in a few mills such as Langford Mill at Kingswood, although most were only active in the throwing process. All of the Stroud silk mills restricted their operations to throwing.

The other part of the county particularly engaged in this trade was the area around Blockley, long a detached part of Worcestershire, and Chipping Campden. Here, the dozen or so mills gradually shut down, the last one closing its doors in the 1880s. As the industry in Blockley dwindled, silk throwing in the Stroud valleys blossomed. Possibly, one prospered at the expense of the other. As Stroud came into the trade later than Blockley, the industry in the former may have been able to capitalize on newer and more efficient throwing equipment.

Apart from the woollen mills in the Stroud valleys, other important mills were also found in and around Wotton-under-Edge, Alderley, Charfield, and Kingswood. However, as the nineteenth century wore on and in the face of increasingly difficult markets, these mills gradually succumbed. Some were turned over to other uses while others were simply demolished.

One of the county's speciality trades that also made use of wool was the manufacture of carpets. Although not carried on in Gloucester on a large scale, at least one major manufacturer (the Gloucester Carpet Company) was active in High Orchard, near Gloucester Docks. Here, in 1915, William Jones, a Kidderminster man, set up his carpet manufacturing business in the vacant Southgate Mills. Initially producing blankets for the war effort, the company later began production of Axminster, Chenille and other types of carpets. Gradually the company expanded and in 1945, under new ownership, the company moved to new premises in High Orchard where it was eventually taken over by the Youghal Carpet Group.

Carpets and rugs were also made in Dursley for a time and, more importantly, in a former woollen cloth mill at Thrupp, near Stroud. Here, the carpet-making concern of Thomas Bond Worth & Sons set up shop, eventually also occupying another site nearby. The mill continues in commercial activity, spinning yarns of different types for the company's main carpet-making plant in Stourport. Many of the fine old buildings are still used.

Cotton never featured highly in the region's past, apart from one major concern situated in Bristol. At Barton Hill on the eastern edge of the city stood the sizeable Great Western Cotton factory, built in 1838 and closed in 1920. Apart from this one company, there was little else in the way of cotton manufacturing in the area.

One of the main replacements for more traditional types of cloth came with the development of nylon in the 1930s. As manufacturing techniques and materials were further developed, this versatile range of synthetic textiles gradually ate into the markets of silk, cotton and wool. In the mid-1950s, nylon production came to prominence in Gloucestershire with the opening of the huge new British Nylon Spinners (BNS) plant at Brockworth, on part of the site formerly occupied by the Gloucester Aircraft Company. In the process, small chips of nylon polymer are melted and extruded through a metal plate filled with tiny holes (a spinneret). The threads formed are cooled, coated with lubricant and wound on to cylinders. In a subsequent process, the threads are stretched and twisted ('drawtwisting') in order to compact and strengthen them. Since its opening, the Gloucester plant has been operated by BNS, ICI Fibres and latterly, Du Pont. Over the last four decades, millions of miles of nylon thread have been produced for a variety of end uses. The company remains a major employer in the county.

Linked to textile manufacture in the county was the making of clothing. Obviously, virtually every town and village had its tailors and dressmakers. However, by the turn of the present century, a number of enterprises were operating on a much larger scale. In Stroud, the brothers George and Henry Holloway set up what was to become one of the most important wholesale clothing companies in the county. From the middle of the nineteenth century, their premises were in Threadneedle Street where they harnessed the power of a steam engine to drive hundreds of sewing machines. Company expansion eventually saw a move to a new factory in Brick Row, from where they turned out substantial quantities of off-the-peg clothing that was shipped throughout the land. The Brick Row factory remained in use from about 1903 up to the 1980s before it was eventually fire damaged then demolished. The Holloways were not alone in Stroud. In 1898, the firm of Williamson, Tratt & Co. built a large rectangular building that still stands at Cheapside. Within a few years they went bankrupt, but from 1902 the business was carried on by Hill-Paul Ltd who remained there until 1990.

Off-the-peg clothing was also manufactured in Gloucester where a number of companies provided employment for large numbers of, primarily, women workers. For instance, by 1904 the Gloucester Shirt Company in Magdala Road, originally set up in 1882, employed 200 operatives 'whose capacity is greatly multiplied by the best machinery and appliances that modern invention has produced'. The complex of buildings eventually encompassed a steam laundry, ironing rooms, drying chambers, and making-up rooms. Materials came from Britain and parts of Europe, a huge range being kept in stock. A 20 h.p. steam engine provided power for the sewing machines.

An engraving showing Nind Mills near Wotton-under-Edge, *c.* 1900. At the time, this extensive woollen mill was being operated by Millman & Hunt. Power was provided by a combination of steam and three waterwheels worked by the Little Avon. Many grades of fine quality cloth were produced using Australian and German wools.

A group of women workers at Lodgemore Mill, near Stroud, *c.* 1910. One of the few remaining cloth mills in operation, the site has been in use since the sixteenth century. At different times the mill was worked by N.S. Marling and J.G. Strachan. For many years it was run in conjunction with Cam and Longfords Mills.

A group of male workers at Lodgemore Mill, *c.* 1910. The old stone-built mill was burnt down in 1871 and replaced with the present brick buildings designed by local engineer James Ferrabee.

Woodchester Mills, *c.* 1925. The site was in use from the 1600s and accommodated corn and fulling mills before being rebuilt as a factory woollen mill in 1803–4. Steam power was added to supplement water power in about 1830. Clothmaking ended in about 1890.

Dunkirk Mill, Nailsworth, *c.* 1910. This magnificent mill remains as one of the finest reminders of the county's woollen cloth trade. The main building comprises four main blocks, ranging in date from 1798 to 1855. Water power was used initially although a steam engine was added later. The mill was subsequently used for the manufacture of walking sticks, hosiery, and later, engineering. In recent years it has been partially converted to apartments.

It was not unusual for several generations of the same family to be working in the same mill. This helped build a strong sense of community and encouraged workers to participate in many out-of-work activities. Mill sports teams, choirs gardening clubs, for example, existed. This 1930s picture shows the Ham Mill brass band.

Longfords Mill, near Avening, 1950s. From 1759 to 1990, woollen cloth was manufactured here by generations of the Playne family and their successors. The site produced a variety of products and grew to encompass over fifty separate buildings. Power was supplied by combinations of water, steam, diesel and electricity. The huge Gatcombe Lake directly above the mill was created by the Playnes to ensure regular water supplies.

British Nylon Spinners took over part of the former Gloucester Aircraft Company site in Brockworth. Here, in 1959, parts of the original hangars are being dismantled during the site's redevelopment.

The transformation continues apace. This shows the front of the BNS works under construction in 1960.

Staff arriving for work at BNS, 1961. The plant later formed part of a group of factories situated in Pontypool and the north of England. Research and development work was carried out in Harrogate.

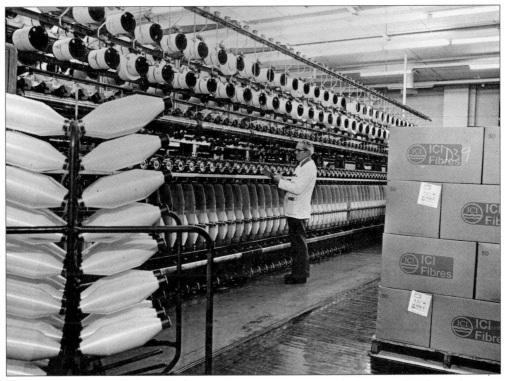

Part of the Drawtwist Department at the Gloucester works in 1971. By now, BNS had been taken over and the site formed part of ICI's Fibre Division. In drawtwisting, loosely spun yarn is stretched and twisted in order to reduce its bulk and increase its strength.

Holloways' clothing factory, Stroud, clearly decked out for a festive occasion, *c.* 1900. Notice the preponderance of women workers engaged on hand processes. However, the overseers were invariably male! Women were cheaper to employ and better suited to tasks requiring a high degree of dexterity.

One of Holloways' finishing rooms, *c.* 1900. Light was at a premium for such detailed work, hence the large windows and gas lights. Note the immaculately turned out women workers and male overseers.

Part of the special order workroom of the Gloucester Shirt Company, 1904. In this room 120 operatives worked, alongside a considerable quantity of high-speed machinery. Despite this, the room was relatively quiet and featured a forced ventilation system.

Langford Mill, Kingswood, *c.* 1904. At the time, this former woollen cloth mill was being used by Messrs Tubbs & Lewis. The company operated several large mills in the region, producing elasticated fabrics, pins and other textile-based products. Langford Mill was used for silk throwing. The company's other mills included New and Abbey Mills.

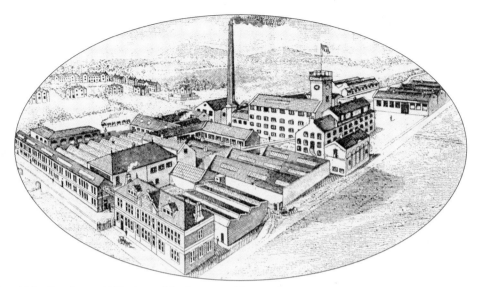

Cam Mills, Dursley, *c.* 1900. One of the largest and longest-lived cloth mills in the region, this extensive mill produced a wide range of woollen cloth types and like so many others in the area, grew piecemeal over many years. At the turn of the century, Hunt & Winterbotham were employing over 400 hands and were engaged in the manufacture of the highest grade woollen cloth. The mills were almost entirely self-sufficient and highly automated from an early date. It continues in use today, as part of the Milliken Group of companies.

In 1900, the woollen cloth-making business of Alfred Ritchie (set up in 1863) was sold to Thomas Bond Worth & Sons, carpet weavers. In its initial stages, the company had 300 carpet looms and employed over 700 local workers. This picture shows the scene in the loom shop in 1928. (FSM Textile Group)

Carpet looms in operation in Ham Mills, *c*. 1910. Note the extensive use of overhead line shafting to take power to the individual looms and other machinery. (FSM Textiles Group)

This shows the mending shop of Thomas Bond Worth & Sons, 1920s. As with many textile-related occupations, women predominated. (FSM Textiles Group)

The boss's office! This rarely photographed scene shows the manager's office at Ham Mills, 1930s. The aptly named Mr Weaver stands on the right. (FSM Textile Group)

For much of its working life, Ham Mills relied on a combination of water and steam power. Here, in 1907, a new Lancashire boiler is being manoeuvred into place using a combination of muscle and a steam crane. Remarkably, the boiler survives and is now used as a water tank. (FSM Textiles Group)

ENGINEERING

For centuries, the City of Gloucester was rightly famous for the quality and diversity of the goods that it produced. Its foundries, iron works and factories turned out many products, ranging in scale from pins to hydraulic machinery the size of houses. Particularly during the nineteenth century, a number of engineering companies developed, often from humble beginnings, into concerns of national and even international repute. Some major firms produced a wide range of components while others developed more specialized lines and services.

In and around the city, a host of engineering and metal-working companies grew up, supplying industries throughout the country. Some, such as foundries, also supplied factories within the city while others manufactured a range of equipment that found its way into regions further afield. Some major engineering companies of note included Summers & Scott, the Gloucester Carriage & Wagon Works, W. Sisson & Co., Williams & James, Kell & Co., and J.M. Butt & Company. Many others operated on a more modest scale, both in Gloucester and in the towns and villages of the county. The products of the latter were frequently aimed at meeting purely local needs.

Some major companies, such as Summers & Scott, operated as general engineering concerns, producing anything that was asked of them. Others specialized in certain types of manufacturing. For instance, Sisson's built their reputation on the production of 'patent high speed engines for dynamos, and high class marine machinery'. Another speciality line was to develop at the Atlas Works of Fielding & Platt. Starting out as general engineers, they gradually moved into the specialized area of hydraulic engineering, producing machinery and components, often of incredible longevity, that were sent throughout the world. Several Gloucester companies came to specialize in making machinery for flour mills, gradually developing into major international suppliers. In Stroud, Excelsior Engineering of Bowbridge built a range of steam engines and the Dudbridge Iron Works developed a range of gas and oil engines. Thus, throughout the more industrialized parts of the county, iron founders and engineers of varying size operated, either meeting the needs of other local manufacturers or exporting their wares the length and breadth of the nation.

Many engineering firms developed in the immediate area around Stroud and in the valleys. Some grew out of the ranks of millwrights, blacksmiths and machine makers who had made their livings servicing and supplying machinery to the innumerable cloth mills of the region. A number of these concerns remained fairly modest in size and specialized in one or two areas, while others, in the wake of cloth-making's gradual decline, expanded and developed new markets for their products. For instance, the successful engineering company of H.J.H. King of Nailsworth produced a range of innovative equipment and steam engines. Some was aimed at meeting the needs of the local trades and industries while other specially developed machinery was sold to maltings and coal mines, both in Britain and abroad. Alongside the likes of the King company, other household names such as Daniels Engineering of Rodborough, the large Waller factory situated on the site of the Phoenix Ironworks, and the Dudbridge Iron Works all turned out wide ranges of industrial and agricultural equipment destined for many markets.

In the southern part of the county, the important Lister-Petter empire, still the main employer in the Dursley area, had its roots in both the cloth trade and agriculture. Ashton Lister's first tentative steps were taken with the founding of his company in Dursley in 1867. From this modest start, the company gradually grew, encompassing the manufacture of cloth-making machinery, milling equipment, cream separators, churns, sheep-shearing equipment and more importantly, the development and manufacture of a range of diesel engines that would make the company a household name throughout the industrialized world.

Overall, engineering and its related trades played a major role in the history of the county, eventually ensuring that its products were to be found both throughout Britain, and in some cases throughout the world.

The extensive works of Williams & James, adjacent to Chequers Bridge, Gloucester, 1940s. The company came to specialize in compressors and related products, such as spraying and vacuum plant. Williams & James was founded in about 1915, a wartime period that saw the expansion of a number of county engineering firms. Production of compressors continues under the Hamworthy banner.

One of the innovative pieces of equipment developed by Williams & James during the 1930s was this engine-driven air compressor, used for inflating car tyres. It seems unlikely that it was pursued to full commercial production.

Just to confirm that nothing is new. This picture shows a Williams & James pressure washer system in use outside the main factory building, *c.* 1930.

Clearly a busy place: the main Williams & James factory workshop, 1950s. Notice the preponderance of lathes, mills and drilling machines, etc. Some are powered by dedicated electric motors and others by traditional overhead line-shafting.

Pressure reducing valves being assembled in the Williams & James factory, mid-1950s. Great care was always taken in the selection of suitably skilled staff for this type of work.

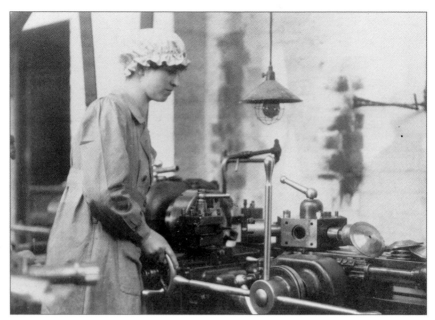

During both world wars, many normal activities came to an end and mills and factories were turned over to war work. During the First World War, many mills and engineering works in the Stroud region, such as Newman, Hender & Co., became important centres for the manufacture of shell components, fuses, etc. Here, a young woman operates a lathe producing shell parts, a job that only a few years earlier had been an all-male preserve.

The manufacture of munitions was often a skilled and sometimes dangerous job. As so many men were away in the trenches, women took their places in packing and assembling shells in the hope that it would help ensure the safe return of their loved ones. This group is thought to have been at work in the Stroud area.

During the early 1940s, work started on the construction of a large new engineering works in Stonehouse. Here, the ball-bearing manufacturing company of Hoffman Engineering built their extensive factory on a piece of swampy land adjacent to Oldends Lane. In this picture, the shell of the main workshop has been partially completed while a crane prepares the ground for the new office block. Clearly, the manufacture of bearings was crucial to the war effort.

Here, the concrete footings of the Hoffman works are being laid, ready for construction of the rest of the building. Very deep footings were required because of the swampy nature of the ground. Notice how little mechanical equipment is in use.

The power house under construction at the Hoffman site. A spur from the LMS railway line nearby allowed supplies of coal to be brought directly to the boilers. Once open, the works relied initially on labour imported from Middlesex and Essex.

An eerie light hangs over the almost deserted Hoffman factory in this wartime night picture. As with many other production facilities at the time, overhead line-shafting took power to many of the machines. Production still carries on in these workshops under the RHP Aerospace banner. The company is now part of the NSK Group and retains an international reputation for the manufacture of ball and roller bearings for engine, aircraft and other specialized applications.

Some of the most important aspects in engineering were actually involved with daily maintenance. This scene shows the maintenance workshop at Ham Mills, near Stroud, then in use for carpet weaving. Most mills and factories were, by necessity, largely self-sufficient in terms of repairs and maintenance. (FSM Textiles Group)

For many years, one of the largest and most important engineering firms in the Stroud region was Newman, Hender & Co., located in Woodchester. First established in 1879, the company survived in various forms until 1994. They specialized in the manufacture of valves used for many industrial processes. This picture shows the extensive works in 1953. (FSM Textiles Group)

From small beginnings, Newman, Hender & Co. grew to a company of international repute. This picture from the 1880s shows the original base of operations in the old Dyehouse cloth mill at Woodchester. Samuel Newman started his small engineering business here in 1879. He later amalgamated with Frank Hender, brass founder and finisher. Notice the old wool drying tower on the right.

At the turn of the century, Newman, Hender & Co. were described as manufacturers of 'engine fittings, boiler mountings, gun metal and iron cocks, and valves of every description for engineers, boiler makers, shipbuilders, etc'. This 1904 picture shows part of the finishing and assembly shop.

High pressure testing of Newman-Milliken valves, *c.* 1950. These valves were an important part of the company's overall production.

Part of the Newman, Hender & Co. bronze foundry, 1953. In the foreground, pouring operations are taking place on a gravity track. Machine moulding is taking place at the rear. (FSM Textiles Group)

A general view of the Newman, Hender & Co. machine shop, packed with capstan and turret lathes, 1953. (FSM Textiles Group)

Electrical engineering also featured highly in the county's past, primarily in the shape of Mawdsley's Ltd of Dursley. The company was set up in Rivers Mill, previously occupied by Lister's and used for pin manufacture. Mawdsley's started producing rotating electrical machines in 1907 and by the 1970s had customers in over fifty countries. This shows an early Mawdsley generator mounted on a steam traction engine.

Listers, Dursley, c. 1945. For the past century, the name of Listers has been synonymous with Dursley. Robert Ashton Lister moved from Yorkshire in the 1860s and began producing cloth-making equipment. He soon added agricultural equipment, and from 1909 they started production of their world-famous range of engines.

Workers in Sir Ashton Lister's 'old' Dursley foundry. This started operations in about 1910 and worked up to 1939 when a new foundry took over. On Friday 17 November of that year, the 'bottom was dropped' for the last time out of the cupola in the old works. It had worked continuously throughout this period, producing castings for a wide range of the company's products.

A general view of the old foundry, September 1931. Notice how labour-intensive the work was. This was to change with the adoption of new technologies.

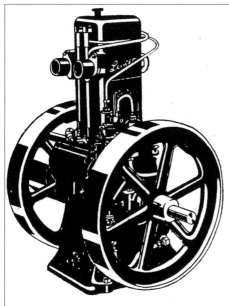

LISTER'S
All British

DIESEL, PETROL
and PARAFFIN
ENGINES
for all purposes.

ELECTRIC
LIGHTING PLANTS.
PUMPING PLANTS.
TILLAGE
IMPLEMENTS, etc.

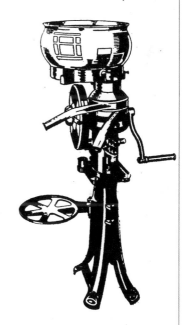

CREAM SEPARATORS
and other
DAIRY MACHINERY.

IRONMONGERY
of Every Description.

County Representatives of
ALFA LAVAL
MILKING MACHINES.

Free Estimates and Lists.

R. A. LISTER & Co., Ltd.
Engineers and Ironmongers,

STATION ROAD : GLOUCESTER.

Established 1867. **Telephone 2358.**

An advertisement of 1926, indicating the range of products being manufactured in the main Dursley works and the various offshoots in different parts of the county.

A 3-ton capacity oil-heated Hote receiver, forming part of the Lister's foundry's B Track in 1959.

Lister's foundry in full swing, late 1950s. In later years, engine manufacture attained a dominant role, with innumerable castings being produced to meet the requirements of an increasingly international market-place.

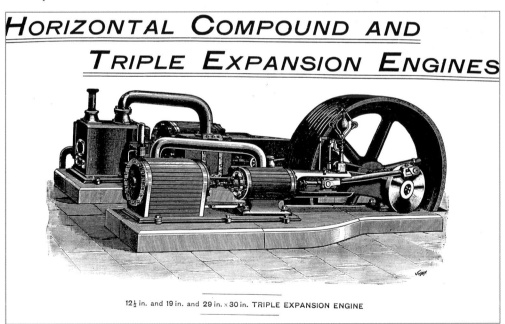

HORIZONTAL COMPOUND AND TRIPLE EXPANSION ENGINES

12½ in. and 19 in. and 29 in. × 30 in. TRIPLE EXPANSION ENGINE

The engineering company of H.J.H. King was set up in Nailsworth in about 1875. From here the company operated as general and mill engineers and developed a series of innovative designs of steam engine. They also produced agricultural machinery, water turbines and equipment for maltings. This plate shows one of their range of steam engines. From the 1880s, the company installed their engines in a number of local mills and factories, and updated older engines from other manufacturers.

Entrance to Redler Conveyors works, 1948. After the large Dudbridge cloth mill closed in 1933, it was taken over by Redler Conveyors Ltd, formerly situated at Sharpness Docks. The company specialized in the development and manufacture of malting and bulk-handling equipment such as conveyors, storage and feeding systems. The company still occupies this site.

Redler's original base of operations was at Sharpness. This picture from about 1900 shows their large steam-powered Elysium flour mill at the docks.

Redler's general assembly shop, *c.* 1948. Known for a time as the 'Ready Built Works', Redler Conveyor's Dudbridge factory produced a range of bulk-handling equipment used for moving large quantities of grain, coal and other products.

Redler's assembly line, 1948. It was used for the production of steel trunking needed for the manufacture of all types of 'Ready Built' conveyors. Using a modular approach, conveyor systems could be tailored to meet individual customer's needs.

The manufacture of coal-handling equipment formed an important part of Redler's business for many years. This 1940s advertisement shows a coal boiler and handling system, typical of many commercial and industrial installations of the time. Redler coal handling plant could be highly automated and was capable of feeding coal to both stoker and pulverized coal-fired boilers under conditions of great cleanliness.

One of the largest engineering companies in Gloucester was the Gloucester Railway Carriage & Wagon Works. First opened in 1860, it eventually closed in the 1980s. From its huge site, many innovative products were shipped to railways throughout Britain and overseas. This picture shows the world's first all-iron railway waggon, displayed at the London International Exhibition of 1862.

'City of Gloucester' coach, 1890s. Not all of the company's products were purely practical in nature; they also produced a number of luxurious passenger coaches. In order to show their skills to the world, this appropriately named coach was built specifically for important exhibitions. The company later built similar coaches for overseas royalty, such as the Maharajah of Indore.

Automatic couplings under test at Gloucester, January 1887. The tests were to assess the effectiveness of Richard Hill's patented design.

Car manufacture never ranked highly in the county's industrial past although in the early part of the century, the Gloucester Light Car Company and the Carriage & Wagon Works produced small numbers. Of greater longevity was the Hampton Car Company, an emigré from Birmingham, situated in the industrial hamlet of Dudbridge, near Stroud. From 1920, hand-crafted saloons and roadsters were built. However, the company was unable to withstand the competition from the large mass producers such as Austin, and closed in 1932.

The county's smallest registered manufacturer was George Stevens, proprietor of Pitts Garage in Gloucester. He built this stylish special for his own use. The car used a one-off chassis, clad with a steel and aluminium body and was powered by a hybrid engine. Total 'factory' output was one! The car successfully competed in many sporting trials in the late 1940s and early 1950s.

Staff of Cales' No. 2 Factory in Harbour Road, Lydney, early 1950s. The company produced only lacquered hair pins which were exported far and wide. It was later bought out by the Whitecroft Pin Company and was eventually taken over by Neweys, a Birmingham-based manufacturer. Mrs E.M. Reynolds is present in this group; she started there shortly after the end of the Second World War and was the factory's fastest pin packer.

A workshop at the Stroud Metal Company, *c.* 1900. Originally set up in 1899, the company specialized in brass founding and the production of umbrella fittings. The latter were supplied to a number of local umbrella manufacturers. In addition, the works produced a wide range of components including steam and water valves and gauges, and brass components for electrical and motoring uses.

The firm of W. Sisson & Co. was set up in 1889, following the takeover of an earlier engineering business. The company operated initially as general and marine engineers but later came to specialize in the production of their own design of patent high-speed steam engines destined for boats and dynamos. Despite these specialities, in the 1920s they built chocolate-rolling equipment for Cadbury Brothers. This 1950s picture shows Frederick Howell (on the right) at work in the pattern-making shop.

The Phoenix Iron Works, Thrupp, near Stroud, 1911. Surrounded by the tools and products of their trade, these workers are engaged in wedding festivities. Several appear to be drinking from chamber pots! From 1851, the business was carried on by the Ferrabee family, producing cloth-making machinery, corn milling equipment, waterwheels and steam engines. The first lawn mower and adjustable spanner were also made here.

Some of the many workers employed by the Gloucester Aircraft Company at its main site at Brockworth, 1930s. At its peak, the company's highly skilled workforce numbered in excess of 14,000. Most worked at the main site although others operated in forty smaller departments scattered throughout the county.

Gloucester Aircraft Company woodworking shop, Brockworth, c. 1935. GAC's factory and out-stations were ultimately capable of producing virtually anything from wood or metal. From their workshops, large numbers of fighter aircraft, including the country's first jet aircraft, emerged over a period of nearly half a century. During lean periods, the company rented out hangars and other buildings for non-aviation uses.

The end of an era. The last Meteor (WL 191) was built by GAC in 1954, ending a production run of eleven years. The last Meteor (shown here) left the site on 9 April 1954. In 1961, GAC was merged with Whitworth Aircraft and later became part of the Hawker Siddeley empire. The site was finally closed and sold off in 1964.

For over half a century, Smiths Industries at Bishops Cleeve has remained one of the most important specialist manufacturing companies in the county. Up to 1969, the company, famed internationally for its aviation instrumentation, operated its own fleet of specially equipped aircraft, used for development purposes. Here, at Staverton Airport is the 'Smiths' Flying Unit' comprising Proctor, Avro XIX and Dakota.

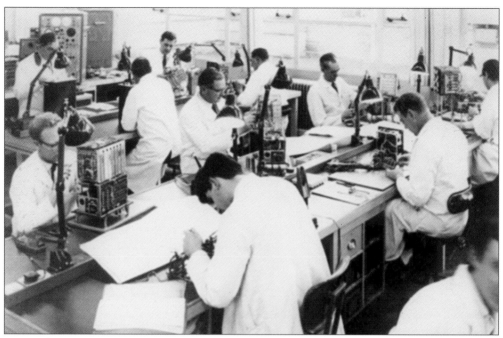

An important range of products manufactured by Smiths consisted of autopilot systems, developed to allow aircraft to land in conditions of limited visibility. 'Autoland' systems were first adopted for commercial airline use in the 1960s. Much testing and development was carried out using Smiths' own aircraft. Here, SEP 5 autopilots are being assembled under conditions of clinical cleanliness.

In order to train and educate staff to the high standards required, the company opened its own Technical School in 1951. Here, workers were trained to become highly skilled designers, tool makers, production engineers, etc. The school was equipped with a full complement of the latest engineering equipment. This picture from the late 1950s shows a selection of fitting and turning benches.

Permali Ltd, new site, 1955. One of Gloucester's important manufacturers has long been Permali Ltd. Set up originally in 1937 as the New Insulation Company, the company specialized in the development and production of insulating materials and components. From small beginnings in the former tram depot in Bristol Road, the company expanded greatly over the passing years. In 1956, work started on the construction of a large new factory across the road.

A scene in the old East Works (the former tram depot) in the 1940s, showing the production of paper bushings used in the manufacture of high voltage switchgear and transformers.

Many of Permali's insulating products were made from layers of thin wood veneers, impregnated with resins and bonded together under heat and pressure. These were then machined into the appropriate forms. The company imported veneers from France via Gloucester Docks. Here, a load of beech veneers is being unloaded from the *Kon Tiki*.

Not all veneers were imported as the company also produced considerable quantities from its own works. This 1950s picture shows the machine used to peel thin sheets of veneer from rotating beech logs. This was housed in Permali's Ashleworth factory.

A Fielding & Platt 250-ton stretch-forming machine, used for the manufacture of aircraft components, 1940s. During the Second World War, such company-built equipment worked round the clock at several aircraft factories including those of the Bristol Aeroplane Company and Fairey Aviation Ltd. Stretch-forming presses were used for the manufacture of wing leading edges of Spitfires and Hurricanes.

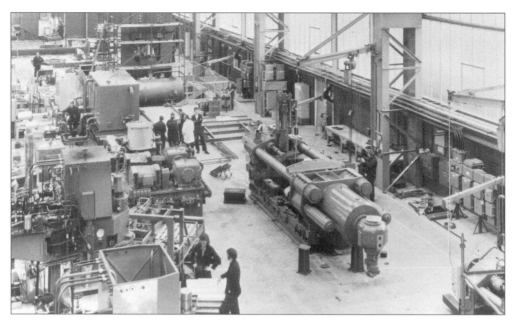

The main assembly shop of Fielding & Platt's Atlas works in the 1970s, showing a number of hydraulic presses and ancillary equipment being built. Fielding & Platt equipment has long had a reputation for quality and reliability, with many products operating trouble-free for decades.

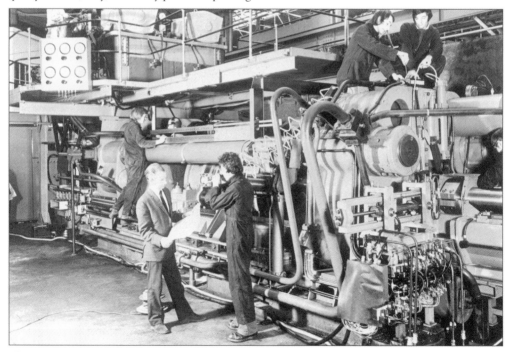

The Gloucester-based engineering company of Fielding & Platt have operated from the same site since 1866. During this time they have produced a wide range of machinery destined for many applications. From 1871, the company began to specialize in the development of hydraulic engineering, an area in which they remain internationally famous. This mid-1960s picture shows a 1,600-ton horizontal hydrostatic extrusion press, used for extruding aluminium sections.

SHOPS & SERVICES

By its very nature, the following section comprises a miscellany of trades, professions and industries. Many were common to all parts of the country. Wherever people lived, many workers made their livings meeting the needs of their peers. Jobs ranged from one-man operations, through small shops and manufactories, to large country-wide activities such as the supply of water and the delivery of the daily post. As with the changing face of the county's industries, the typical shop has altered in both its appearance and function with the passing years. For example, a trade brochure from 1925 listing the shops in Stroud concluded that even though the town was well stocked with a variety of outfitters, chemists, grocers, food suppliers, etc., other opportunities were still available. It noted that 'Firms specially needed in the town [were] An Exclusive Hatters, A high-class Cafe with Orchestra, and A multiple firm of Tailors'. The situation continues to change from year to year.

A common scene in many parts until relatively recent years. The general ironmonger's shop stocked a huge array of tools, building fitments, gardening materials, and general household requirements such as oil lamps and cutlery. Austin's shop in Worcester Street, Gloucester, shown here in 1924, also specialized in supplying and installing plumbing and gas fittings.

Miles' shop, Eastington, c. 1910. The typical village shop had to cater for many needs and frequently sold a bit of everything! Miles' shop doubled primarily as draper and grocer. In addition, it acted as the post office, housing the first telephone in the village. The shop is still in use.

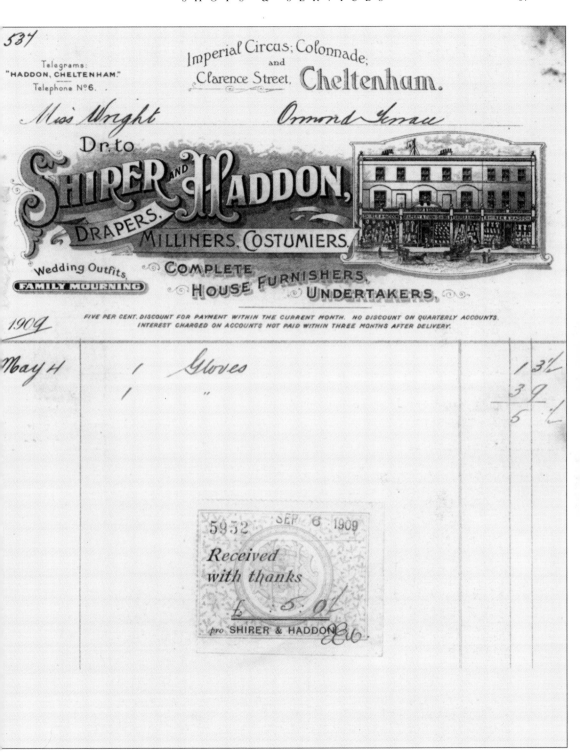

537

Imperial Circus, Colonnade,
and
Clarence Street, **Cheltenham.**

Miss Wright   *Ormond Terrace*

Dr. to

SHIRER AND HADDON,

DRAPERS.

MILLINERS, COSTUMIERS.

Wedding Outfits.   COMPLETE

FAMILY MOURNING   HOUSE FURNISHERS, UNDERTAKERS,

FIVE PER CENT. DISCOUNT FOR PAYMENT WITHIN THE CURRENT MONTH. NO DISCOUNT ON QUARTERLY ACCOUNTS.
INTEREST CHARGED ON ACCOUNTS NOT PAID WITHIN THREE MONTHS AFTER DELIVERY.

1909

May 4	1	Gloves	1	3½
	1	"	3	9
			5	½

5932   SEP 6 1909
*Received
with thanks*
£   5   0½
pro SHIRER & HADDON

A far cry from the village shop were the up-market emporiums of fashionable Cheltenham. Here, speciality shops catering for the wealthier segments of society flourished. This invoice from Shirer & Haddon of Imperial Circus and Clarence Street, dated 1909, was for two pairs of gloves.

One of the new breed of multi-purpose shops built for the Gloucestershire Co-operative Society. This one was built in lower Barton Street during the 1930s by the Gloucester-based building firm of J.B. Halls & Sons. In later years it became the home of the Co-operative's funeral services, a role it continues to fulfil.

A busy scene in Barton Street, *c.* 1960, showing the variety of shops and small businesses that once lined both sides of the street. The railway crossing is behind the photographer.

The butcher's shop of Thomas Keck in Southgate Street, Gloucester, *c.* 1960. The lights strung across the road and the turkeys hanging in the window suggest that Christmas is approaching. The building's medieval roots are evident as it stands squashed between later constructions. It is now the SPCK bookshop.

From Victorian times, the milk roundsman was a common sight, plying his early morning wares in the streets of cities, towns and villages throughout the land. Many were essentially one-man affairs although in the case of William Eldridge of Hucclecote, other family members assisted with his round. This picture shows the complimentary calendar issued to larger and more favoured customers. At this time, milk was delivered by horse-drawn float.

Some businesses combined selling from a shop with a delivery service. Such was the case with Hone's bakery in Eastington. The bakery, with Mr Hone in the doorway, stood at Millend. Deliveries were sent around the area by waggon and handcart.

Also a familiar sight in the county's towns was the local coal merchant. Most had their own rounds and obtained their bulk supplies from the nearest stockpile, usually supplied by rail. This scene shows deliveries being made in Cheltenham by Messrs Nealon & Sons.

At the turn of the century, Gloucester boasted the unusual Glevum Manufacturing Works of Roberts Brothers. Here, they invented and produced a variety of indoor games, puzzles, picture cubes, and 'ABC Blocks'. The works were built in 1902, and housed woodworking, cardboard box making, wire-working, painting and varnishing departments. Production was necessarily very labour-intensive. This picture shows some of the workforce outside the front of the works.

Not all selling of wares occurred in shops. Here, Eldorado ice cream is sold from a suitably modified tricycle. A regular sight in Whitminster and along the A38, this ice cream seller had regular stops such as the Whitminster café.

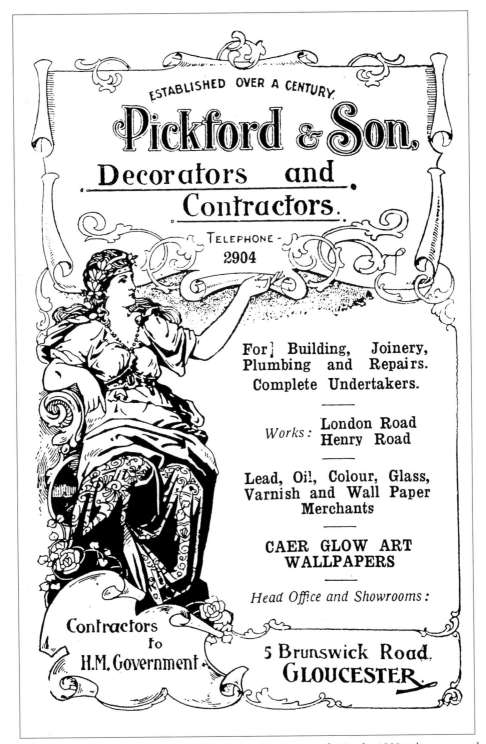

The Pickford company had many of its roots in the canal carrying trade. By the 1920s, the company had numerous branches, one of which was engaged in a range of building and decorating activities. This attractive advertisement dates from 1925.

The Christmas mail arrives at a snow-bound Drybrook in the Forest of Dean, *c*. 1930. At this time, mail was sent by train to Drybrook station; this closed in the 1930s and road transport took over. Head Postman Walter King is the central figure looking left. Four postmen served the area. Mr Cowmeadow, on the right, ran Drybrook post office.

Postman Cliff Mills stands beside his mail van in Prince Street, Gloucester, *c*. 1960. Some of these rugged vans had rubber wings to minimize damage in the event of a collision. Cliff was the regular postman for the Minsterworth area for several decades.

A busy day in Howard Street, Gloucester, c. 1910. Here, council workmen are hard at work installing new sewer pipes. It appears that the entire local population has come out to watch. Notice the little girl, dressed in her Sunday best, posed on the spoil heap.

A further pipe-laying exercise, this time in High Street, Tredworth, c. 1915. Notice the complete lack of machinery, operations relying solely on manpower and simple tools. Clearly a labour-intensive way of working, as there are no fewer than twenty workers in view.

The Water Board's works at the Mythe near Tewkesbury, *c*. 1936. In the foreground is Telford's ornate toll house associated with the adjacent cast-iron bridge spanning the Severn. The works supplied drinking water to a wide area of the county.

On occasions, notable dignitaries were present in the county. Here, Aneurin Bevan, Minister of Health, is attending the opening of the Water Board's Leathern Bottle Reservoir, 10 October 1950.

This picture from 1953 shows Water Board employees being 'delivered' to work. They are engaged in the construction of a pipe tunnel under the River Avon near Tewkesbury.

Two cranes and many Water Board employees were engaged in the construction of the Mill Avon pipe bridge, near Tewkesbury in 1953.

TRANSPORT

Before the railway network reached the county, the most important means of transporting goods was by water. For centuries, the River Severn formed the major route, and at certain times of the year was navigable as far upstream as Stourport, Welshpool and Ironbridge. Gloucester was the hub of much water-borne trade and served as an important crossing point over the Severn.

From the latter part of the eighteenth century, canals began to have an impact on the county's transport system, with the opening of the Stroudwater Canal in 1779, followed by the 29-mile long Thames & Severn in 1789. On the other side of the county, the 34-mile Hereford & Gloucester Canal gradually made its way towards Hereford, construction starting in 1793 and continuing until 1845. Several smaller canals were also built. The Pidcock family, ironmasters of the Forest of Dean, cut a canal between their iron works and Lydney Pill, and at Coombe Hill, near the Cheltenham–Tewkesbury road, a short broad canal ran from Wainlode on the Severn to a basin at the foot of the hill. It was intended as a route for bringing coal to Cheltenham, although financially it proved to be a disaster.

Many of Gloucestershire's roads formed important through routes, although at certain times of the year some were virtually impassable. Improvements began with the formation of the turnpike trusts, the first one opening in the county in 1698. Over the ensuing fifty years, this was followed by many others, leaving behind a legacy of distinctive milestones and toll houses along important routes. Turnpikes were eventually de-piked, largely as a result of the increasing competition from the railways. The canal trade also suffered for the same reason.

During the nineteenth century, several important rail links arrived in the county. In 1840, the Birmingham & Gloucester Railway reached Gloucester and Cheltenham, and in 1844, the Bristol & Gloucester Railway was opened. These and several other companies and schemes were eventually subsumed into the larger Midland and Great Western companies. Some of the more important railway schemes in the county included the Cheltenham & Great Western Union Railway, the South Wales Railway, the Banbury & Cheltenham Direct Railway, the Severn Bridge Railway, the Severn & Wye Railway, the Midland & Southern Western Junction Railway, and the Stonehouse & Nailsworth Railway. Some, such as the latter, were primarily aimed at meeting local needs.

For almost a century, the City of Gloucester remained an important railway centre. Up to the cessation of steam operations in the mid-1960s, the city had two rail depots: the Horton Road Depot, opened in 1872, formed part of the GWR network, and the Barnwood Depot belonged to the Midland Railway. Sadly, most of the city's once-proud railway heritage was swept away in the 1960s and '70s.

Apart from the main lines running throughout the county, in pre-Beeching days, there were many branch lines linking previously isolated towns and villages. In addition, particularly in the more industrialized areas, numerous branches and spurs linked mines, quarries, brick works, mills and factories directly with the main rail networks. In most places, few traces now remain.

One of the first cars (AD 1) in the Stroud area belonged to Revd George Thomas Altimus Ward, vicar of Eastington from 1903. He was noted as 'an experienced traveller, man of the world, and a brilliant conversationalist' as well as a pioneer motorist.

The Stroudwater Canal was built between 1775 and 1779, providing a lifeline to the many mills and factories in the Stroud valleys. Here, a barge makes its way along part of the Eastington section towards Pike Lock and bridge, c. 1910. This part of the canal rose through a series of five locks. The canal company's main dry dock and a coal yard (on the left) were mid-way along this section.

Brimscombe Bridge, Thames & Severn Canal, *c.* 1910. This typical humpback structure carried the road from Minchinhampton to Brimscombe. Behind is the Ship Inn, one much used by canal boatmen.

Brimscombe Port was the headquarters of the Thames & Severn Canal Company. It functioned primarily as the transhipment point between narrow Thames barges and the bulkier Severn trows. In front of the company headquarters, shown here in about 1910, was a large basin which could reputedly hold up to 100 vessels. The building housed a warehouse, offices and agent's house. It later became Brimscombe Polytechnic, an education and training establishment, and was finally demolished in 1964.

Boats inevitably required repair and maintenance and in Gloucester, one of the boatyards catering for the needs of river and canal boats was run by William 'Shiner' Price and his sons. The yard stood downstream of Westgate Bridge and over many years, repaired the boats of most of the major local river and canal carriers. Shiner was a well-known local character who carried on working until well into his eighties.

Both water and road transport occasionally came to a stop in Gloucester, as a result of the tricks of the Severn. In 1915 the Quay was inundated, stopping boats and closing various roads and bridges. It also shut down many of the workshops that lined the road. The circular building in the distance is the lower section of the seventeenth-century glasshouse, used for the manufacture of bottles, jars and glasses.

At a time when most people still relied on their feet, this farmer wends his peaceful way through Newnham, 1907. Powered road transport was still a relative rarity, especially in rural areas.

The advent of the bicycle opened up new horizons for many people. No longer were they limited to their immediate locale. The pattern of work for many also changed, as longer daily distances now became viable. Here, in the 1890s, Miss Gilbert, the district nurse, prepares for her round in the north Cotswold area.

Steam traction played an important role up to the early part of the present century, especially for moving large, heavy loads. Perhaps one of the most unusual loads to be shifted was this small house, being relocated in Hucclecote, 1928. The building was 30 ft x 17 ft.

With the increasing popularity of the private car, new opportunities arose. Apart from the wayside garage, new eating places sprang up, tailored for motor traffic. At Whitminster, on the Bristol Road, a former wheelwright's shop was converted to a café and tearoom, run by the Jones family, 1931–41.

The all-important cook in the café was Mrs Nellie Jones.

Although popular with motorists, the café was also a useful staging post for lorries en route from the Midlands to the West Country and elsewhere. Here, a laden steam lorry poses alongside more regular callers.

A Wolseley Wasp in the foreground, again outside the café.

As motoring increased during the 1930s, so the problems of finding the best route and obtaining assistance at the roadside grew. Help often came in the form of the AA man. Here, Hughie Jones mans his box at the fork in the road outside the Cross Hands pub at Quedgeley. The bike was his means of transport.

In later years, Hughie was given his BSA motorcycle and sidecar in order to assist with the inevitable breakdowns that were a common feature of the early days of motoring. Eventually, an AA minivan met this need. Hughie served the AA for many years.

One of the Leyland lorries belonging to haulage contractor W.J.B. Halls of Gloucester, early 1920s. The company's base near Barton Gates was later to develop into one of the most important builders' merchants in the city.

A train of charabancs lined up outside the carpet works of Thomas Bond Worth & Co. of Stroud, 1920s. The company also had works in Stourport and Kidderminster and held inter-works sports days. This outing is possibly one of these occasions. From 1954, the Stroud works became the spinning centre for the Stourport factory. (FSM Textiles Group)

An Albion lorry of Halls the builders, Gloucester, early 1930s. The pristine condition suggests that it is new, as builders and builders' merchants trucks inevitably had a hard working life.

A happy day for all post-war motorists. The staff of Higgs & Nibletts Garage in Coleford celebrate the end of petrol rationing. Notice Chad's comment of 'Wot No Coupons'.

As motorized transport increased in popularity, small wayside garages carrying out repairs and selling tyres, oils and petrol proliferated. Sometimes, they grew out of former blacksmiths' businesses. This group of intrepid motorists post outside the premises occupied by Western Garages in the once-rural location of Ebley, near Stroud, *c.* 1925.

Eastington Garage (1947) developed out of Law's small wayside cycle shop (shown in the background), which had been added to the front of an existing cottage early in the century. Like many rurally located examples, in its earlier days, the garage met both local motoring and agricultural needs.

Strettons Garage, Worcester Street, Gloucester, *c.* 1925. They were agents for Morris, Cowley and Oxford, Buick, Austin and Daimler cars. There was also a branch at the Bell Hotel in the city.

A wet day in the late 1950s at Pitts Garage in Barton Street, Gloucester. Originally set up in about 1936 as a small repair garage, the business was systematically built up by the managing director from 1945, George Stevens. In 1948, he took on the Lea Francis agency and held this until the marque finally disappeared. From 1956 to 1972, Pitts was the main Renault dealership for Gloucestershire and Herefordshire and later became agents for Datsun. George Stevens remained the owner up to his retirement in 1997.

By the end of the 1950s, Permali Ltd was making many of its deliveries using a fleet of vans. Larger components and deliveries went by company lorry.

These stout fellows formed one of the LMS plate-laying gangs at work in the county, *c.* 1900. On the left is Harry Grinnell, foreman plate-layer, who died as a result of injuries suffered while working. He was reputedly carried in a wheelbarrow to his home in Quedgeley, where he died of a 'cerebral haemorrhage, the result of a sprain in carrying on his work'.

A network of lines eventually spread throughout much of the formerly inaccessible Forest of Dean. Many were linked to coal mines and other industrial enterprises. Others linked the numerous small settlements and towns in the region. This picture shows the Dean rail motor service at Steam Mills Crossing, *c.* 1910.

The Lydbrook viaduct, *c.* 1920. This impressive masonry and iron structure carried the Severn & Wye Railway's connection between Lydbrook and Serridge Junction. It continued to bestride the valley until its demolition in the 1960s.

In 1965, following the closure of many of the lines in and out of the Forest of Dean, the Lydbrook viaduct came to the end of its life. The demolition men moved in and removed one of the most prominent reminders of the region's industrial past. The massive iron spans were dismantled and lowered to the road for eventual removal. (From the collection of the Dean Heritage Museum Trust)

High above the rooftops of Lydbrook, one intrepid demolition worker slices away metal with a cutting torch. (From the collection of the Dean Heritage Museum Trust)

A Midland Railway Deeley 4–2–2 hurries its train through the cutting known as 'The Gullet', near Stonehouse, en route to Bristol, *c.* 1900. The line originally formed part of the Bristol–Gloucester railway, opened in the 1840s.

Gloucester was an important railway centre for much of the nineteenth and twentieth centuries. The city had both GWR and LMS depots. This photograph shows the GWR 85B Horton Road Depot in 1960. Castle and Grange locomotives are in view.

MILLING

From time immemorial, small-scale milling was carried out in virtually every corner of the county, often in small water-powered mills set up wherever there was sufficient water available. Small corn mills housing one or two pairs of millstones became a feature of the local landscape where, for hundreds of years, they ground locally grown cereal crops, almost exclusively for local consumption. Mills often belonged to the lord of the manor or were tied to a religious order, villagers were normally obliged to have their corn ground at a particular mill.

Few significant changes occurred in the layout and configuration of the country mill for hundreds of years, although, especially as the nineteenth century progressed, their overall number gradually declined. Surviving mills got bigger and often, through the use of water power augmented with a steam engine, their output increased markedly. In many places, millstones gave way to newer developments such as roller mill systems. However, these traditional ways of working came under increasing threat from the large, steam-powered mills set up in and around Gloucester Docks and at Tewkesbury. Increasingly, the country miller found himself unable to compete with these large milling companies. In an effort to stay afloat, some switched to producing animal feeds, although usually it only delayed the inevitable. By the middle of the present century, the country mill had all but disappeared, with only a handful soldiering on producing animal feed beyond the 1950s.

Milling flour was now exclusively in the hands of a few large milling companies. In Gloucester, Priday-Metford came to dominate the trade, while in Tewkesbury, it was Samuel Healing's huge mills by the banks of the river. Capitalizing on the inexpensive and rapid transport of grain via the Gloucester–Sharpness Canal and Gloucester Docks, these milling companies were able to sweep away any serious remaining local competition.

Although Priday-Metford's mill finally closed in the 1990s, Healing's mill still continues to thrive, its nineteenth-century buildings housing some of the most advanced milling equipment in Europe.

Stowell Mill was typical of the innumerable small country mills that dotted the county's landscape. This mill belonged to the Stowell Park Estate and spent most of its long life grinding corn from the estate's farms. A very old working site, it was one of three mills noted in Chedworth Manor in Domesday Book. The mill ceased operations around the time of the Second World War. An iron breastshot waterwheel drove two pairs of millstones.

The village flour mill at Lower Slaughter, *c.* 1950. Powered by the Eye Brook, from the 1870s until the mill's final closure in the 1940s, it was run by successive generations of the Wilkins family. Power for the mill's two sets of millstones was provided by an iron breastshot waterwheel, augmented (from about 1914) by a small steam engine. In later years, it served as the village baking business of A.C. Collet & Sons. It is now a small museum.

Bourton Mill, *c.* 1910. The mill was worked by the Wilkins family from 1840 until after the Second World War. The attractively sited mill was powered alternatively by water, steam, oil and gas engines. It was fairly large for a country mill and in 1893, roller milling equipment replaced the millstones. The West Midland Farmers used the building from 1950 until 1974. It now houses a motoring and village bygones museum.

Bledington Mill, *c.* 1920. This was a typical village corn mill, found throughout the county wherever suitable streams were present. Supplying predominantly local customers, the mill was powered by the Westcote Brook and worked successively by the Harris, Hadley and Simms families. It ceased operations in the 1940s.

One of the largest and most productive mills in the county was that established in 1865 by Samuel Healing near the confluence of the Rivers Avon and Severn in Tewkesbury. The company made use of the river for water-borne transport of grain to the mill, although it relied initially on horse-drawn waggons and later, steam power for road deliveries. This is one of the company's early Foden steam lorries.

By the 1930s, steam had given way to the petrol engine. Here, some of the Healing's fleet of delivery lorries are lined up outside the magnificent mill buildings. Remarkably, this classic nineteenth-century exterior now contains some of the most sophisticated milling plant in the world.

Samuel Healing's original mill was extended in 1889 although, as with any substantial industrial building, alterations inevitably took place regularly. Here, in 1960, steeplejacks are busy removing the top 90 ft from one of the mill's stacks.

Up to relatively recent times, grain continued to be brought to Healing's Mill by water, the company's fleet of five barges carrying grain from Avonmouth, Sharpness and Gloucester. The barges had a carrying capacity of 225–320 tonnes. A unique discharging system comprising several chain link conveyors unloaded the grain directly into the mill's silos.

The Phillpotts, Kimberley, Herbert, Vinings and Sturges warehouses, *c.* 1910. Most of the cereals used by the major Gloucester millers arrived via the canal and Gloucester Docks. From here, huge quantities of wheat, barley, maize and oats were either milled locally or sent on to other destinations. Up to twenty of the large warehouses ringing the docks were used to store imported grain at some time.

One of the longest-lived flour mills in the City of Gloucester was that of Priday, Metford & Co., adjacent to the docks. First established in 1850, the mill was advantageously sited for easy access to grain brought in via Sharpness and Gloucester Docks. From small beginnings, a series of expansions and modernizations ensured that the company remained an important Gloucester miller until the early 1990s.

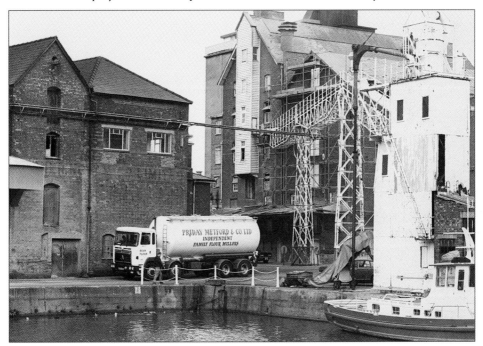

Towards the end of its working life, the Priday, Metford mill no longer relied on moving grain and flour by boat. By the 1980s, road tankers were fulfilling these tasks. The gantry leading to the mill formed part of the unloading system designed to transfer grain directly from boats into the mill's silos.

The Managing Director's private office, Turner, Nott & Co., Gloucester, *c.* 1900. This important corn merchant also had premises in Bristol, its Gloucester base consisting of a large six-storey warehouse, with a capacity for 30,000 sacks of grain. There was also a kiln house and offices. Grain was imported from many countries.

The Turner, Nott & Co.'s premises in Gloucester, *c.* 1900. Much of the grain imported by the company was either sold locally or sent on to locations throughout the Midlands. The company also manufactured its own brands of cattle and horse feeds.

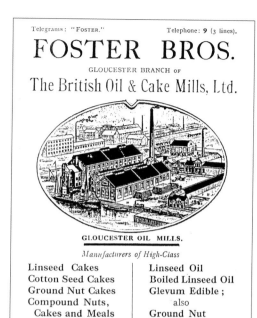

Milling in Gloucester was not limited to flour. Foster Brothers operated as a branch of the British Oil and Cake Mills Ltd from a large mill in the docks where they produced a range of animal feeds and oils derived from ground nuts and linseed. Many of their raw materials were imported. This advertisement dates from 1925.

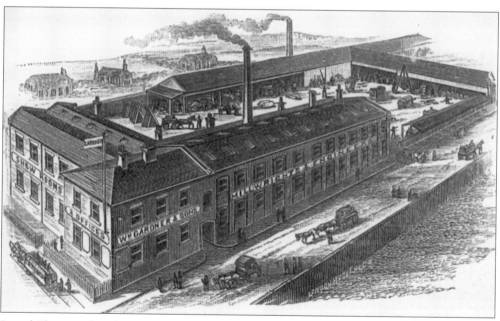

Several Gloucester-based companies specialized in the manufacture of milling equipment, one of the most important being that set up by William Gardner in about 1860. Initially based in premises in Llanthony Road, he later settled in a large new works on the Bristol Road. The company made a wide range of flour milling machinery, roller mills, dressing machines, sifting machines, driers, and millstones. The business continued in various forms up to recent years. This illustration shows the Bristol Road works in about 1910.

The turning and fitting shop at Gardner's works, *c*. 1890.

The Gloucester company of Simon-Barron became one of international repute in milling circles. Originally set up in works at Ladybellgate and Kingsholm by Mr W.S. Barron, the firm came to produce a wide range of milling and grinding equipment, much destined for flour mills. In 1932, the works were relocated to a new 7-acre site along the Bristol Road. In 1934, links with Henry Simon's company were established and Simon-Barrons Ltd was created. This picture shows the millstone manufacturing shop, 1920s.

AGRICULTURE & THE RURAL CRAFTS

As noted earlier, the county splits into three distinctly different regions and each was characterized by different uses of the land. In the Severn Vale, agriculture revolved around a mixture of arable and pasture land, plus fruit growing and dairying. In the Forest of Dean, not surprisingly, timber growing reigned supreme although where appropriate crops were grown and sheep kept. On the Cotswold uplands, sheep were formerly kept in huge numbers and cattle were grazed, the latter mainly on the lower-lying land. In addition, land was used to grow crops including peas, potatoes, beans, wheat, turnips, vetches, swedes, oats, barley and grasses.

In the county's agricultural areas, partially as a result of their relative isolation and traditional ways, numerous craft industries survived. Many of these were carried on by particular families, the skills being passed down through successive generations. For instance, along the banks of the Severn were families skilled in making nets and fish traps, while in other regions, craftsmen wove baskets and made traditional farm hurdles. Thus, some skills were regional and others were to be found throughout the county. In the latter category, perhaps the thatcher had a pedigree of almost unparalleled longevity. He was responsible for roofing houses, barns and hayricks, the same family sometimes working in the same village for generations. Sadly, most of these highly skilled craftsmen are now no more than local memories, although a handful continue to earn their livings much as their forefathers did.

Haymaking remained a universal theme throughout the centuries. In this 1920s picture, a single horse provides the only addition to muscle power on fields at Ebley near Stroud, now long submerged under housing developments.

Haymaking at Eastington, *c.* 1910. This was very much a family affair, with everyone pitching in. Often, other occupations were abandoned until haymaking was over.

A peaceful scene in a time of war. Haymaking on the Lydney Park Estate, May 1941. (From the collection of the Dean Heritage Museum Trust)

Silage making at Ellery's Tutshill Farm, early 1940s. The farm horse was still a common sight at this time, especially in petrol-starved Britain. (From the collection of the Dean Heritage Museum Trust)

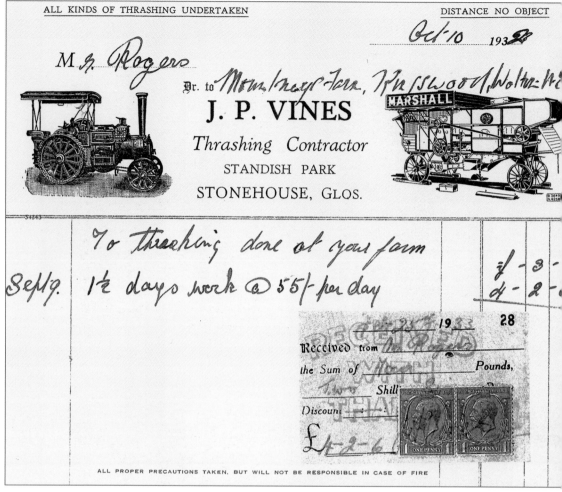

ALL KINDS OF THRASHING UNDERTAKEN

DISTANCE NO OBJECT

Oct 10 193*2*

M*r* *Rogers*

Dr. to *Mountnags Farm, Kingswood, Wotton...*

J. P. VINES

Thrashing Contractor

STANDISH PARK

STONEHOUSE, GLOS.

MARSHALL

Sept 9. | To thrashing done at your farm
1½ days work @ 55/- per day

Received from
the Sum of
Two Shill
Discount
£4-2-6

ALL PROPER PRECAUTIONS TAKEN, BUT WILL NOT BE RESPONSIBLE IN CASE OF FIRE

It became increasingly common for farmers to call upon the services of the specialist contractor. Here, the thrashing contractor J.P. Vines is invoicing a Kingswood farmer for thrashing carried out at the owner's farm, 1932.

Among the work of rural craftsmen, that of the thatcher was often rated as one of the most skilled. This picture from about 1930 shows Jack and Fred Cale (up ladders) working on the roof of Reeds Farm, now the Little Thatch restaurant at Quedgeley. Mr Williams, the owner, stands on the extreme left. Thatching was carried out using traditional long straw as opposed to reeds.

Fred Cale, working on a roof, was eighty years old when this picture was taken in 1941. Particularly in the 1920s and '30s, the Cale family was famous for its thatching skills and was responsible for roofing cottages, farms and ricks within a 25-mile radius of the workshops in Quedgeley. Fred also doubled as the village grave digger – his rate was 2s 6d a hole!

Thatching was difficult during the bad winter weather and Fred Cale turned to basket making during the off-season. He was followed by his son, Jack, and in turn, by Jack's son, Richard. Richard continues as one of the few skilled master basket makers still active in the trade. The Cales made many variants of baskets. Here, Fred Cale is making an eel trap. He worked at Quedgeley for over seventy years.

Fred Cale's son, Jack, surrounded by some of his beautifully made wares, 1951. Between them, the Cales produced thousands of fruit baskets for Pershore and Gloucester markets. It was possible to make up to eight per day, selling for 2s each. As Fred passed his skills on to Jack, so Jack in turn passed on his to his son, Richard.

Although it did not employ huge numbers, the craft of charcoal burning was carried on in various wooded parts of the county until relatively recently. For instance, in some of the wooded areas around Stroud and Cranham charcoal burning was carried on from at least the 1700s until the present century. In particular, this craft was carried on in the Forest of Dean. This is charcoal burner Alfred 'Pat' Roberts at work in the Forest. (From the collection of the Dean Heritage Museum Trust)

Two gardeners and a horse struggle to mow a carpet of buttercups that form part of the lawns at Eastington House, 1932. Originally built as The Leaze by wealthy millowner, Henry Hicks, later influential occupants included the Stanton, Marling and De Lisle Bush families.

Large country houses were often occupied by the squire or, later, a wealthy industrialist. In either case, the owner provided work for many local people, either as servants or working on the grounds and estates. Work was thus provided by Major De Lisle Bush who kept the Eastington beagle pack, here exercising by Westfield Lock on the Stroudwater Canal in 1937. Tom Smith leads with Wilf Hancock bringing up the rear.

POTTERIES

At one time, the small country pottery was a relatively common sight, supplying down-to-earth products for surrounding towns and villages. As transport systems improved, many found themselves trying to compete directly with the large potteries in the Midlands and gradually, most faded out of existence. The country pottery was often small and sometimes relied on locally sourced clays whereas the large potteries of the industrialized Midlands could make use of an enormous range of materials and decorative effects such as transfer printing. Huge tonnages of these products were moved throughout the land by rail and sold by commercial travellers to shops and individual houses. In the face of such competition, the days of the country pottery were essentially numbered. Very few survived after the First World War. Some turned to producing specialist wares in an effort to stay afloat. Such was the case with the small pottery operated by William Moulton in Cranham. Clay dug from local woods was used to produce a range of 'cottage' crockery, flower pots and drainpipes, mostly sold in Gloucester. The business, like so many others, succumbed in the early part of the present century. The only survivor of the country pottery in Gloucestershire is the Winchcombe Pottery.

The present Winchcombe Pottery had its roots in Becketts Pottery, a country works that employed a dozen men. At the time, the kiln was fired weekly, with products being taken by waggon as far as Stratford market. It was taken over by Michael Cardrew, former apprentice to the noted potter, Bernard Leach. Cardrew was responsible for reviving English slipware that had, at the time, virtually disappeared. Here, he is throwing a pot at Winchcombe, *c.* 1934.

A few of the original workers were at Winchcombe when Cardrew took over. One was the wonderfully named Elijah Comfort, shown here at work in 1937.

In 1936, Ray Finch joined Cardrew as an apprentice. Cardrew left in 1939 to start Wenford Bridge Pottery in Cornwall, and Ray took over Winchcombe Pottery. He is shown here setting the bottle kiln at Winchcombe, *c.* 1939. In the pottery's early days, the kiln was fired three or four times a year. It was of the updraught design and had four firemouths.

Sydney and Charles Tustin also worked at the pottery for many years, Here, Charles is firing the bottle kiln, *c.* 1948.

Ray Finch throwing a pot at Winchcombe Pottery, *c.* 1948. Ray's son, Michael, joined the pottery in 1968 and now manages it. The pottery continues to make traditional hand-thrown stoneware. The kiln is wood-fired with gas as backup.

MINING & MINERALS

There were innumerable small coal pits and drifts working in the Forest of Dean at one time, most employing only a few freeminers. In general, pits were relatively shallow and were rarely viable once the water table had been reached. With the introduction of steam-powered pumping, pits could be sunk deeper and kept free of water, allowing increasing exploitation to take place. As the nineteenth century progressed, the number of pits increased dramatically. In 1840 there were around 70 pits and this had risen to 221 by 1856. Between them, they produced some 460,000 tons of coal. The two largest and most mechanized pits were Lightmoor and Parkend, which between them produced around 174,000 tons per annum. Both worked the Middle Series seams at various depths. By the turn of the present century, the Forest's pits were producing around 1,200,000 tons each year. The output from different pits and seams was often destined for different end-uses which included house coal, gas-making, and steam coal.

As pits became deeper, the problems associated with the ingress of water increased. This, accompanied by seams that varied greatly in thickness, did not help balance the account books and inevitably there was a trend towards fewer, much larger pits. The last of these finally closed in 1965. Today, surprisingly little remains above ground as a reminder of this once thriving and important Forest industry. Ironically, only small concerns operated by a handful of freeminers still continue in operation.

Sydney Scott, chief engineer of Trafalgar Colliery, at Serridge Green in the Forest of Dean, 1890s. This pit was the first in the Forest to adopt electric power (1883), the plant consisting of a Gramme machine on the surface, driven by the steam engine, plus a Siemens dynamo used as a 1.5 h.p. motor, belt-driving an underground pump. Despite the relative success of the installation, the adoption of electric power in the Forest's pits remained a slow business. After the pit's closure in 1925, the engine was taken to Cardiff Museum.

Up to fairly late in the present century, the horse still played an important role in parts of the Forest of Dean. Here, William Hobbs is shoeing one of the pit horses at Waterloo Colliery in the 1920s. Both Hobbs and his father formerly owned their own blacksmith's shop in English Bicknor.

The Forest of Dean mining regions were not always places of harmony and during the miners' strike of 1926, the Gloucestershire Constabulary Mounted Police were on hand to keep the peace. The first strike occurred at Trafalgar Colliery. (From the collection of the Dean Heritage Museum Trust)

A typical Forest of Dean scene from between the wars. Here, at Parkend, spoil heaps and winding gear tower over houses and farmland. In many industrialized parts of the Forest, railways, pits and factories were jumbled together in close proximity to villages and workers' housing.

Work in many of the Forest's pits was hard and sometimes dangerous although gas was not generally a problem. As with pits in the country's other mining areas, methods of extraction were laborious and relied heavily on manpower. In this 1930s photograph, Mr Bowdler, a ripper, is at work in the Starkey Seam of Lightmoor Colliery, trimming loose pieces of rock from the roof, following firing with shot. This was to increase working height and allow the passage of loaded waggons. (From the collection of the Dean Heritage Museum Trust)

Miners preparing to move a train of waggons, Lightmoor. A generous working height is evident in this part of the pit. (From the collection of the Dean Heritage Museum Trust)

Miners using an electric coal cutter in a cramped seam in Lightmoor Colliery. Electric cutters were first introduced into the pit in 1937. (From the collection of the Dean Heritage Museum Trust)

An apparently relaxed scene underground at Lightmoor, 1935. Mines Rescue Leader 'Lion' Bowdler sits on an air drill. Notice the crude pit prop, undoubtedly hewn from the forest above. (From the collection of the Dean Heritage Museum Trust)

A 1950s scene at one of the larger of the Forest's pits, then under the control of the National Coal Board. Simple hand tools still operated alongside more sophisticated equipment.

This picture (*c.* 1950) helps to emphasize the difficult conditions sometimes encountered in some of the narrower seams of the Forest's pits.

Lydney Harbour, *c.* 1900. From 1810, the Severn & Wye Railway and Canal Company developed Lydney as a port, primarily to export Forest coal to a variety of destinations which included ports along the Bristol Channel. Much also went along the Stroudwater Canal to the Stroud valley mills. At Lydney, a new canal was cut to the Severn and a tidal basin added in 1821. By the 1890s, Lydney's annual coal trade amounted to 265,000 tons. Coal arrived by rail and was transferred to boats via truck-tipping mechanisms.

A lorry-load of coal arrives at the Coal Research Establishment, Stoke Orchard, for testing purposes, *c.* 1964.

Stoke Orchard, near Cheltenham, *c*. 1960, an incongruous location for a site of national importance to Britain's mining industry. From 1948, the Coal Research Establishment (CRE) carried out research into many coal-related matters. These included the development of smokeless fuels, crucial in the elimination of smog in cities. Initially set up in a redundant Second World War aircraft construction/repair facility adjacent to the Stoke Orchard aerodrome, for half a century great strides were made in producing gaseous and liquid fuels from coal, and in reducing emissions from industrial plant and power stations.

In the wake of the oil crises, strenuous efforts were made to produce oils, transport and aviation fuels from coal. Here is one of the teams engaged in developing a process to derive liquid fuels from coal. Most staff at CRE were skilled engineers and scientists. CRE had a worldwide reputation for its work but was essentially abandoned by the government in its race to close down much of the country's coal industry.

Stone was quarried extensively, especially in the Bixslade area of the Forest of Dean. This valley begins on high ground near Coleford and stretches some 2 km to join the Cannop valley. Stone has been worked here since before the fifteenth century. In later years, huge blocks of Dean stone were hauled along various tramways that snaked through parts of the Forest. The Cannop–Bixslade tramway continued in use up to 1946. In 1860 there were seventeen main quarry workings recorded in Bixslade. (From the collection of the Dean Heritage Museum Trust)

PIANO MANUFACTURE

This specialized craft has been practised by only a handful of makers in the county. Of these, two were very small affairs and short-lived, and one was, and remains, a maker of international importance.

In the village of Blockley, two manufacturers operated for a time. Both were small concerns staffed by family members plus a few hired workers. John Ocock, a woodcarver, and his son ran one of these businesses, making perhaps no more than a handful of pianos during their working lives. In effect, their pianos were individually handmade items. The situation was similar with the firm of Evans & Evans of Sleepy Hollow Mill in Blockley. Both firms appear to have worked from the 1890s up to about 1910.

The only piano maker of any scale to operate in Gloucestershire was the Stroud Piano Company, now the Woodchester Piano Company. They first occupied the redundant Woodchester cloth mill in 1911, when Douglas Grover, a third generation piano maker, arrived from London in the company of ten key workers. Rapid expansion followed and throughout the 1920s and '30s, thousands of various types of pianos were sold. By the 1930s, the company was one of Britain's largest producers. The old mill was destroyed by fire in 1938 but production continued in alternative premises. Since 1945, over half the factory's production has been exported. Since the company first opened its doors in Woodchester, over 160,000 pianos have been built.

Stroud Piano Company's machine shop, 1927. These machines transformed raw timber into finished components. At one time, power was supplied by a steam engine used in conjunction with a water turbine.

A battery of three belt sanders used to smooth the surface of timber parts.

Some of the employees of the Stroud Piano Company, 1927. In the centre is the company's special delivery van, capable of holding nine pianos.

The company's key-making department, 1927. Here, the machinery is electrically driven.

The cramping machine, used to hold pieces of components together during gluing. This ingenious device contained twelve sets of revolving cramps. By the time the eleventh one was loaded, the twelfth was ready for emptying.

Sawing timber on a circular saw. Nine different species and thicknesses of wood were used in a piano's construction. All was kiln dried to ensure stability.

A stage in piano assembly. Typically, a piano contains around 6,000 parts. Around 4,500 of these are found in the action.

CONSTRUCTION & BUILDING TRADES

Construction and building were clearly universal trades. For centuries, every village had its builder, often a local man who was responsible for building and maintaining cottages, barns and houses in the vicinity. From the nineteenth century, it was not uncommon for the local building firm to encompass virtually all of the skills required to put up a cottage or house from scratch. The firm frequently comprised a small core of craftsmen and artisans skilled as masons, carpenters and sometimes thatchers, although more often the latter skill remained in the hands of a few families who had specialized in this trade for generations. The local builder/carpenter was usually a resourceful and multi-talented individual. In truth, he had little choice in the matter. Thus, he often sourced his own timber from local woods, sawed it in his own saw-pit, and after appropriate seasoning, used it in the construction of cottages, making gates and coffins, and building carts for the local farmers. Sometimes his skills also ran to blacksmithing, and he would also build and repair iron-rimmed wheels for the carts and waggons he had built.

As the nineteenth century wore on, the local building firm still maintained a high degree of versatility and remained capable of most tasks required in the building line. Most villages were still relatively isolated and this ensured that the builder, wherever possible, continued to rely on locally available materials. Gradually, as transport and communications improved, it became increasingly possible for the builder to work further afield and to obtain his bricks and timber from some distance away. Specialization increased and in the towns, builders' merchants developed, acting as a centralized source capable of meeting many of the builders' needs. No longer did the village builder have to make his own ironwork or commission the blacksmith to make it. Similarly, he no longer fired his own bricks, quarried his own stone or burnt his own limestone to make mortar. Increasingly, it became a simple matter of a trip to the nearest town.

In some cases, the builders' merchants had grown out of a building firm and in others, carpentry or haulage. Some continued to be active in house building as well as supplying other builders, and grew into sizeable construction companies which were equally capable of building a garden shed or a grand public building. Several important Gloucestershire companies still thriving today developed in this manner.

The building and builders' merchant company of Halls & Keck was an important and active concern, responsible for much building and repair work in the city, 1930s. Their original yard was adjacent to Barton Gates, a site now covered by the B & Q store. A variety of buildings and sheds housed a huge variety of construction materials.

A scene of activity at the Stonehouse Brick & Tile Works, 1959. These works were originally set up in 1890, to make use of the clay deposits of Doverow Hill. The deposits comprised Yellow Plastic, Brown Marl, Blue Lias and Metford Sands, all of excellent quality. By 1904, annual capacity amounted to some 10 million bricks. Later in its life, the works was taken over by a consortium of three builders' merchants who continued to operate the works, primarily to meet their own needs.

The building firm of W.J.B. Halls Ltd was established in 1919, becoming Halls & Keck from the mid-1960s. The company was active throughout much of Gloucestershire for many years, in both building and maintaining properties. This scene from the late 1950s shows remedial work being carried out on Foyles shop in Gloucester.

The sawmill of the builder/merchant W.J.B. Halls Ltd, *c.* 1960. Timber working formed an important part of any builder's portfolio. Some firms relied on the city's various sawmills for their supplies whereas others carried out at least some timber-working in-house.

One of the most important construction contracts undertaken by W.J.B. Halls during the 1940s was the construction of the new Gloucester Technical College in Brunswick Road. Here, the site has been cleared, foundations have been completed and work is proceeding on laying the lower courses of bricks.

By April 1940, much of the building had been completed and work now continued apace to complete the landscaping of the surrounding area.

The builder was expected to be able to turn his hand to any task. Here, roofing repairs are taking place at a branch of the Midland Bank, 1937.

The building company of W.J.B. Halls built new houses and also carried out work on older notable properties. An example of the latter included work carried out on the old façade of the Midland Bank at Gloucester Cross, February 1941.

The date is May 1928 and this thatched Tuffley farmhouse is getting new roofing timbers and a dormer, courtesy of W.J.B. Halls Ltd. The company was very versatile and capable of working on property of all ages.

The Davis family of Taynton was typical of the many multi-talented village builders of yesteryear. The company engaged three or four men whose skills included carpentry, wheelwrighting, ladder and gate making, and coffin manufacture. Timber was sourced locally and laboriously sawn in their own sawpit. Sawing was predominantly a winter pastime, when bad weather precluded outdoor work. Here, in the 1890s, a youthful James Davis holds the top of the saw. He was later to perish in the First World War.

The Clutterbuck family of Eastington were also typical village builders. They tackled virtually all aspects of building and maintenance work around the village, including working on local woollen cloth mills. In addition, they also made coffins in their workshop, as shown here, c. 1915.

ACKNOWLEDGEMENTS

Thanks are due to many individuals, organizations and companies, all of whom freely gave of their time, loaned photographs or provided information for this book. This project provided an excuse to contact old friends but also introduced me to many new ones throughout the county and beyond. A considerable debt of gratitude is owed to all of these. Of particular help were the following:

Mrs E. Alder, Martin Beauchamp and Paul Smith of RHP Bearings, Howard Beard, Mr A.D. Brazington, British Coal Corporation, Peter Brown, Mr F.R. Cale, Peter Christmas, Joy and Barry Cresswell, Sue Curran, Mark Daniell of Permali Gloucester Ltd, Mr C. Evans of Joseph Griggs & Co., Carol Evans, David Evans and John Brown of the Dean Heritage Museum Trust, Ray Finch of Winchcombe Pottery, Mr J.M. Fivash of Quaker Chemicals, Mr P.C. Freke of The Woodchester Piano Company, Mr B.R. Gabbett of Redler Ltd, Joan Gay, Wilf Hancock, Roger Hawkes of Fielding & Platt Ltd, Mrs B. Jones, Mrs C. Jones, Sue Jones, Tony Jordan and Sue Howells of Du Pont (UK) Ltd, Jeremy Keck of SWJ Group Ltd, Ian Mackintosh, Bob McLaren, Otto Mellerup, Wilf Merrett, Janice Morris, The National Waterways Museum, Mr R. La Porta of Carpets of Worth, Mrs H. Prickett, Les Pugh, Nick Redman of the Whitbread Archive, Mrs E.M. Reynolds, Pierce Riemer, Severn–Trent Water Ltd, Chris Smith of Hamworthy Compressor Systems Ltd, Paul Starr of Lister-Petter Ltd, Mr J.B. Stephens of Smiths Industries, Mr & Mrs G. Stevens, Harry Townley, Ruth Williams, Mr & Mrs R. Vaile, Mary Wood of Allied Mills.